# FARM JOURNAL'S

## Homemade Ice Cream and Cake

*Delectable Dessert Recipes
from Good Country Cooks*

# FARM JOURNAL'S

## Homemade Ice Cream and Cake

*Delectable Dessert Recipes from Good Country Cooks*

Edited by
### Elise W. Manning
*Farm Journal* Food Editor

By the Food Editors of
### Farm Journal

Galahad Books • New York

First Galahad Books edition published in 1997.

Galahad Books
A division of BBS Publishing Corporation
386 Park Avenue South
New York, NY 10016

Galahad Books is a registered trademark of BBS Publishing Corporation.

Published by arrangement with Doubleday, a division of Bantam Doubleday Dell Publishing Group Inc.

Library of Congress Catalog Card Number: 96-79834
ISBN: 0-88365-997-2

Printed in the United States of America.

# Contents

# FARM JOURNAL'S

## Homemade Ice Cream and Cake

*Delectable Dessert Recipes from Good Country Cooks*

# DO STOP BY FOR HOMEMADE ICE CREAM AND CAKE!

Warm hospitality and sharing food have always been a great part of farm families daily living. Whether it be a neighborly greeting "Stop by for a cup of coffee" or a spur of the moment invitation to stay for dinner, there is sincerity and welcome in their gesture. Their kitchens are country "exchanges" for good food. No matter how busy or harried they are, farm families still seem to have time to think of one another.

Today's city and suburban people also are beginning to realize how important it is to step off the treadmill, and one of the best ways to relax and enjoy friends is by enjoying good food together, rediscovering perhaps that the simple things in life often bring the greatest joy.

A farm woman, for instance, wrote us a warm newsy letter that started: "Happiness is an ice cream freezer—hand cranked, of course. That's important to our family, as we always appreciate the things we work for and wait for, and homemade ice cream is a good example. Everyone from our 8-year-old son to our 75-year-old grandfather wants a turn at the crank." And when the ice cream has churned to smooth velvet someone's sure to suggest inviting neighbors in for a dish heaped high, accompanied by a wedge of feathery light homemade cake.

In this cookbook you'll find the best of hundreds of great country cake and ice cream recipes we have collected, tested and tasted.

# WHO ORIGINATED ICE CREAM?

The first man to sample a frozen dessert was Nero, the emperor of Rome. According to some historians he ordered his subjects to climb mountains, gather up snow and run back with it to the palace. Then he mixed it with fruit juices and flavorings, producing an antique version of today's water ice.

The more prevalent theory gives the Chinese credit for the first discovery of a formula for "ice cream." Marco Polo brought the idea back with him but he added milk instead of water to the mounds of snow, which resulted in a creamier product.

Even in those days a good recipe traveled and eventually "ice cream" came to France. Soon Europe's nobility were being served this new creamy cold dessert.

By the early 1700's the formula had crossed the ocean, but it was still a rare treat in 1809 when Dolly Madison delighted her dinner guests at the White House with ice cream as the grand finale.

The first ice cream factory was established in Baltimore in 1851 by Jacob Fussell, but it wasn't until the 1900's that the ice cream craze swept the country. The ice cream cone appeared in St. Louis at the Louisiana Purchase Exposition in 1904.

Today the United States leads all other countries in the production and consumption of ice cream. We eat more than 700 million gallons a year—about 15 quarts per capita. While there are more than 200 flavors to choose from, about half the ice cream eaten in our country is vanilla. Next choices are chocolate, then strawberry, cherry/vanilla, butter pecan, peach, maple nut and coffee.

## INGREDIENTS AND PROPORTIONS

The basic ingredients in ice cream are cream or milk (whole milk, evaporated or condensed), sugar and flavoring. Ices contain sugar, water and fruit juices. Sherbets can contain milk or water, fruits that have been chopped or puréed, and flavoring.

All types of ice creams are crystalline products and for a smooth creamy ice cream it is important that the crystals be very small. In ice cream, the crystals are simply frozen water or ice. To keep large ice crystals from forming, interfering products are added: butterfat, milk solids, sugar, eggs, fruit and nuts. Fruit juices also help produce a fine-textured ice cream. Gelatin too improves the grain and retards melting, but should only be added in small quantities. Too much results in unpleasant sponginess.

In ice creams that are made by churning, the amount of air whipped in depends on the temperature of the surrounding bath of ice and salt and the rate of speed at which the churn is turned. As the ice melts it absorbs heat from the contents of the inside container and lowers the temperature of the mixture. The temperature is controlled by the salt and ice proportion—a proportion of 8 to 10 parts ice to 1 part rock salt produces a smooth textured ice cream or sherbet. If you add too much salt, the ice cream will freeze too rapidly. You will be unable to continue to turn the handle for a long enough period to incorporate enough air. The result will be a rough grained ice cream.

## ICE CREAM FREEZERS

Ice cream freezers are made of wood, plastic or fiber glass. All produce ice cream but some plastic models are not too well insulated and not as sturdy as the wood or fiber glass. Inside the bucket is a canister containing a metal dasher. The dasher remains stationary while the canister turns.

There are electric mixers and hand-crank types. While the electric is easier to operate, many farm women tell us that part of the joy in making homemade ice cream is family participation—everyone gets a chance to turn the crank, though if there's a strong-armed man around he does the bulk of the churning.

## FREEZING AND RIPENING ICE CREAM

1. Scald freezer can and dasher.

2. Pour the chilled ice cream mixture into the freezer can. Fill can two thirds to three fourths full to leave room for expansion. Fit can into freezer; follow manufacturer's directions if using an electric freezer.

3. Adjust the dasher and cover. Pack crushed ice and rock salt around the can, using 8 to 10 parts ice to 1 part rock salt. Turn the dasher slowly until the ice melts enough to form a brine. Add more ice and salt, mixed in the proper proportions, to maintain the ice level.

Turn the handle fast and steadily until it is hard to turn. Then remove the ice until its level is below the lid of the can; take the lid off. Remove the dasher.

4. To ripen the ice cream, plug the opening in the lid. Cover the can with several thicknesses of waxed paper or foil to make a tight fit for the lid. Put the lid on the can.

5. Pack more of the ice and salt mixture (4 parts ice to 1 part rock salt) around the can, filling the freezer. Cover the freezer with a blanket, canvas or other heavy cloth, or with newspapers. Let ice cream ripen at least 4 hours. Or put the can in the home freezer to ripen.

NOTE: If you buy ice by the pound, you will need about 20 lbs. ice to freeze and ripen ice cream in a 1-gallon freezer.

# CHAPTER 1

# *Vanilla and Variations*

"I'll take vanila" is the most popular response when ice cream flavor preferences are asked. Farm women tell us their friends and families prefer vanilla and that's the flavor that they are most likely to make. They do add fresh strawberries or peaches when they're in season. But every now and then the family hankers for a different flavor so good farm cooks have lots of surprise variations made from their favorite basic vanilla.

There are many different recipes for good old plain vanilla—we have a delicious variety of farm family favorites. Some are rich in heavy cream, others are made with milk and evaporated milk; some are cooked custards, others are uncooked. Many farm women favor evaporated milk because it gives an extra-rich and creamy flavor. For those who keep an eye on calories we have a Frozen Vanilla Custard made with skim milk and it has four yummy variations, too.

There are many ways to dress up plain vanilla. A pour of hot maple syrup adds a sweet note. Thawed orange juice concentrate spooned over ice cream and topped with coconut provides a festive last-minute dessert. A ladling of canned or fresh fruit over a dip of vanilla makes a nutritious as well as attractive ending to a meal. And you'll want to try our sauces (see "Sauces and Toppings").

## COOKED CUSTARD ICE CREAMS

We discovered that every woman has her own favorite recipe for Basic Vanilla Ice Cream. The following recipes have a cooked custard base. And each good cook has her preference as to the number of eggs and the amount of heavy or light cream or evaporated milk—many times the recipe combines all three. You will have to try all our recipes before you decide which one you prefer . . . we liked every one!

## BASIC VANILLA ICE CREAM

*Add a sifting of orange flavor gelatin over each serving*

| | |
|---|---|
| 1½ c. sugar | 4 eggs, beaten |
| 2 tblsp. flour | 1 qt. light cream |
| ½ tsp. salt | 2 tblsp. vanilla |
| 1 qt. milk | |

Combine sugar, flour and salt. Slowly stir in milk and eggs. Cook, stirring constantly, until slightly thickened. Cool.

Stir light cream and vanilla into cooled mixture. Pour into 1-gal. freezer can. Freeze by basic directions (see "Freezing and Ripening Ice Cream" in Index). Makes about 1 gallon.

## CREAMY VANILLA ICE CREAM

*Sprinkle with coconut and add a drizzle of butterscotch sauce*

| | |
|---|---|
| 2 qts. heavy cream | 1½ c. sugar |
| 2 c. milk | ¼ tsp. salt |
| 4 eggs | 1 tsp. vanilla |
| ½ c. sweetened condensed milk (not evaporated) | |

Heat 2 c. cream with milk in top of double boiler.

Beat eggs slightly. Add sweetened condensed milk, sugar and salt. Blend in a little hot cream, then slowly add to mixture in double boiler.

Cook about 5 minutes, stirring, until mixture just coats spoon. Cool.

Stir in vanilla and remaining cream. Freeze by basic directions (see "Freezing and Ripening Ice Cream" in Index). Makes 1 gallon.

## *Variations*

**Chocolate:** Omit 1 qt. cream. Melt 6 squares unsweetened chocolate in double boiler. Blend in ½ c. additional sugar. Slowly stir in 1 c. boiling water. Add to cooked base.

**Peppermint:** Omit 1 pt. cream and vanilla. Add 1 lb. crushed mints and tint with green food color, if you wish, before freezing.

**Coffee:** Omit 1 qt. cream and vanilla. Add 2 c. strong coffee with ¼ c. sugar.

**Apricot:** Omit 1½ qts. cream, 1 c. milk and vanilla. Add 2 qts. mashed apricot pulp, 2 c. apricot juice and 1 c. additional sugar.

**Fresh Peach:** Omit 1½ qts. cream, 1 c. milk and vanilla. Add 2 qts. sieved peach pulp, 2 c. peach juice and 1 c. additional sugar.

**Strawberry or Raspberry:** Omit 1 qt. cream, 1 c. milk and vanilla. Add 2 qts. sieved berries with 1 c. additional sugar.

**Peanut Brittle:** Omit 1 pt. cream and vanilla. Add 1 lb. crushed peanut brittle.

## HOMEMADE VANILLA ICE CREAM

*Velvety, rich, delicious—perfect go-along with your homemade cake*

| | |
|---|---|
| 1 qt. milk | 4 eggs, slightly beaten |
| 2 c. sugar | 1 tblsp. vanilla |
| ¼ c. flour | 1½ qts. light cream, or dairy |
| ½ tsp. salt | half-and-half |

Scald milk. Mix sugar, flour and salt. Add enough hot milk to sugar-flour mixture to make a thin paste. Stir paste into hot milk. Cook over low heat, stirring constantly, until mixture thickens slightly, about 15 minutes.

Add hot mixture gradually to beaten eggs and cook over low heat, stirring constantly, until mixture thickens slightly, about 2 minutes (do not cook longer or eggs may curdle).

Cool quickly in refrigerator. Do not allow mixture to cool at room temperature.

Add vanilla and light cream to cooled mixture. Pour into 1-gal. freezer can; fill only two thirds full to allow for expansion. Freeze and ripen by basic directions (see "Freezing and Ripening Ice Cream" in Index). Makes 1 gallon.

### Variations

**Chocolate Ice Cream:** Add 4 squares unsweetened chocolate to milk before scalding. After scalding, beat with rotary beater until chocolate flecks disappear. Increase sugar by ½ c. and prepare according to directions for freezing Homemade Vanilla Ice Cream.

**Peanut Butter Ice Cream:** Omit 1 c. light cream. Stir a small amount of the custard mixture gradually into ½ c. peanut butter to blend well. Add to rest of the mixture in the freezer can.

**Strawberry Ice Cream:** Omit 3 c. light cream. Add 1 qt. washed and hulled strawberries which have been mashed and sweetened with ½ c. additional sugar. Add a few drops of red food color if you wish.

**Peach Ice Cream:** Omit 3 c. light cream. Add 1 qt. crushed fresh peaches mixed with ¾ c. additional sugar.

## MARIELLA'S ICE CREAM

*A Kansas dairyman's wife freezes this ice cream for Christmas giving*

| | |
|---|---|
| 1 qt. milk, scalded | 1 qt. cold milk |
| 4 eggs, beaten | 2 tblsp. vanilla |
| 2½ c. sugar | ¼ tsp. salt |
| 2½ to 3 c. heavy cream | 3 drops lemon extract |

Stir hot milk slowly into eggs and sugar; cook slowly over direct heat until thickened, stirring constantly; cool.

Add remaining ingredients to cooled egg mixture; stir until smooth. Pour into 1-gal. freezer can. Freeze by basic directions (see "Freezing and Ripening Ice Cream" in Index). Makes about 1 gallon.

## Variations

**Chocolate:** Stir 1 (5½ oz.) can chocolate syrup into vanilla mixture.

**Strawberry:** Mix 3 (10 oz.) pkgs. frozen strawberries, thawed, and ½ c. sugar; stir into vanilla mixture; add red food color for pink ice cream.

NOTE: You can make 4 batches consecutively. By time the custard for the fourth one is cooked, the first is cool enough to put in freezer can. When that gallon is frozen, the second batch is ready for freezing. This assembly line method makes economical use of ice. A 50-lb. bag of cracked ice is enough to freeze 4 gallons. You save time by using the same bowls and pans for each batch. A good selection is to make 2 gallons of vanilla, 1 of chocolate and 1 strawberry.

# NO-COOK ICE CREAM

Many women like the speedy method of making ice cream. No cooking of the custard base is necessary in these ice creams. Just beat the eggs and sugar, mix with the milk or cream and pour into the freezer can. Farm women like to make this type when they are pushed for time and yet want to please the family with home-made ice cream.

## FAST-MIX ICE CREAM

*No cooking of custard—this refreshing dessert tastes like ice milk*

| | |
|---|---|
| 5 eggs, beaten | 1 (14½ oz.) can evaporated |
| 2½ c. sugar | milk |
| 1 tblsp. vanilla | 2 qts. milk |

Mix all ingredients. Pour into 1-gal. freezer can. Freeze and ripen by basic directions (see "Freezing and Ripening Ice Cream" in Index). Makes about 1 gallon.

## SATIN VANILLA

*Pour the cold milk and cream right into freezer—no custard to cook*

| | |
|---|---|
| 4 eggs | 1½ qts. light cream |
| 1½ c. sugar | 1 qt. milk |
| ¼ tsp. salt | 2 tsp. vanilla |

Beat eggs until light and fluffy. Gradually beat in sugar and salt. Stir in remaining ingredients.

Pour into 1-gal. freezer can. Freeze by basic directions (see "Freezing and Ripening Ice Cream" in Index). Makes 1 gallon.

## VANILLA ICE CREAM

*Dress up this ice cream with sundae sauces or chopped toasted nuts*

| | |
|---|---|
| 5 eggs | 1 qt. heavy cream |
| 2½ c. sugar | 2 tblsp. vanilla |
| 5 c. milk | ½ tsp. salt |

Beat eggs until light and fluffy. Gradually add sugar and continue beating until mixture is stiff. Add remaining ingredients and mix thoroughly.

Pour into 1-gal. freezer can and freeze by basic directions (see "Freezing and Ripening Ice Cream" in Index). Makes 1 gallon.

# REFRESHING AND NOT TOO RICH

We give you recipes for two ice creams that taste heavenly but are not rich in heavy cream. Vanilla Ice Cream has a gelatin base—the surprise ingredient is vanilla instant pudding mix. Tastes light and lovely!

Frozen Vanilla Custard made with skim milk is deliciously low in calories and tastes like ice milk. The variations are tasty too. A wonderful dessert to serve those guests who are watching their waistlines. Accompany with fingers of unfrosted sponge or angel food cake.

## VANILLA ICE CREAM

*Refreshingly light ice cream—not too sweet and not too rich*

| | |
|---|---|
| 2 tblsp. unflavored gelatin | 1½ qts. light cream |
| 3 c. milk | 1 (3¾ oz.) pkg. vanilla instant |
| 2 c. sugar | pudding |
| ¼ tsp. salt | 5 tsp. vanilla |
| 6 eggs | |

Soften gelatin in ½ c. cold milk. Scald 1½ c. milk and stir into gelatin mixture until it dissolves. Add sugar and salt, stirring until dissolved. Add remaining 1 c. milk.

Beat eggs at high speed of electric mixer 5 minutes. Add light cream, pudding mix, vanilla, then gelatin mixture.

Pour into 1-gal. ice cream can. Freeze following basic directions (see "Freezing and Ripening Ice Cream" in Index). Makes 3½ quarts.

## Variations

**Grape:** Substitute 3 c. grape juice for milk. Proceed as directed, reducing light cream to 5 c. and sugar to 1¼ c.; omit vanilla. Add the juice of 1 lemon.

**Cinnamon:** Slowly melt ⅔ c. cinnamon (red hot) candies with the 1½ c. milk. Proceed as directed, reducing sugar to 1¼ c. and vanilla to 1 tblsp.

**Coffee Walnut:** Add ¼ c. instant coffee with pudding mix. Reduce vanilla to 1 tblsp. After ice cream is frozen, stir in 1 c. coarsely chopped, toasted walnuts. Repack.

**Peppermint Stick:** Melt ½ c. crushed peppermint stick candy with the 1½ c. milk. Proceed as directed, reducing sugar to 1¼ c. and vanilla to 1 tblsp. After cream is frozen, stir in ½ c. crushed peppermint stick candy; repack.

## FROZEN VANILLA CUSTARD

*Made with skim milk—has fewer calories than many ice creams*

| | |
|---|---|
| 3 qts. skim milk | 8 eggs, slightly beaten |
| 2 c. sugar | 2 envelopes unflavored gelatin, |
| 6 tblsp. flour | softened in ¼ c. cold water |
| 2 tsp. salt | 3 tblsp. vanilla |

Scald milk in top of double boiler. Mix sugar, flour and salt and add a little of the hot milk. Blend well and add to milk in double boiler. Cook over boiling water until bubbles form at the edge of the pan.

Remove from heat. Add the hot mixture gradually to the eggs. Return to double boiler and cook over simmering, not boiling, water, stirring constantly, until mixture coats a wooden spoon.

Remove from the heat; gradually stir the hot mixture into the gelatin, stirring until the gelatin completely dissolves. Refrigerate until custard thickens, about 2 hours, or until it reaches 70°. (You can cook the custard a day ahead and refrigerate it.) Add vanilla to cooled custard.

Pour into 1-gal. freezer can. Freeze and ripen by basic directions (see "Freezing and Ripening Ice Cream" in Index). Makes 1 gallon. (105 calories per ½ cup serving.)

## *Variations*

**Frozen Coffee Custard:** Omit vanilla. Reserve 1 c. custard and add ¼ c. instant coffee. When custard is partly frozen, add coffee-custard mixture and continue freezing until firm. (105 calories per ½ cup serving.)

**Frozen Banana Custard:** Add 5 large, very ripe bananas, mashed (about 2 c.), and ¼ tsp. yellow food color. Freeze. (117 calories per ½ cup serving.)

**Frozen Peppermint Stick Custard:** Add ¼ tsp. green food color to chilled custard. Partially freeze. Add 1 c. crushed green and white peppermint stick candy, or omit food color and add red and white peppermint stick candy; freeze. (125 calories per ½ cup serving.)

**Frozen Strawberry Custard:** Omit 1 tsp. salt and 1 c. milk when making custard. Partially freeze. Add 2 c. sliced, fresh strawberries sweetened with 2 tblsp. sugar. Freeze until firm. (109 calories per ½ cup serving.)

# CHAPTER 2

# *Choose Your Flavor*

After several gallons of Basic Vanilla, it's time to think of a flavor change. Many farm homemakers favor fresh peach ice cream or strawberry, especially if they grow their own fruits. But they also use their imaginations and have shared with us a wonderful collection of other flavors their families favor. Some are unusual and unique, like Orange Pekoe Tea Ice Cream, a combination of milk, cream, eggs, honey and a whisper of tea flavor. For an extra-special treat one farm family makes two freezersful of Golden Glow Ice Cream. Rich in eggs and cream, it tastes and looks golden and is scrumptious to serve at an ice cream social.

Peppermint is a top favorite, too—a pink and white delight with a refreshing sting. For a quick-fix party dessert, spoon homemade peppermint ice cream into parfait glasses, alternating with swirls of chocolate sauce. It's just right with chocolate cake. For a different dessert, bake your favorite chocolate cupcakes, then cool and scoop out the centers and fill with peppermint ice cream. Add a sprinkling of grated chocolate. Delight the children at a birthday party with their very own dessert! Simply spoon peppermint ice cream into paper cups, cover with chocolate "jimmies" or "shots" and plunge a peppermint candy stick in the center—it will make a big hit!

A springtime special is Rhubarb Ice Cream, delicate pink with just the right tang . . . perfect to serve at showers or parties; lovely over a wedge of angel food cake. Coconut lovers will ask for seconds when you dish up Coconut/Honey Ice Cream, smooth and creamy with a delicate taste of coconut.

"Wow, is this good!" That's what you'll hear when you serve Fruited Velvet Ice Cream. Chock full of familiar favorites—nuts, bananas, pineapple, maraschino cherries, and fresh strawberries—this ice cream is a popular family favorite.

Then we have rich Coffee/Walnut, Rocky Road Special, Double Chocolate . . . many more that you'll want to try.

## ESPECIALLY FOR CHOCOLATE FANS

Three delicious chocolate ice creams for the men in the family who say "I like anything as long as it's chocolate." The darkest and richest of them all—Double Chocolate—with both unsweetened and semisweet chocolate in the same recipe. Youngsters will like the pale green chocolate-studded Chocolate Mint.

### DOUBLE CHOCOLATE ICE CREAM

*Top with chocolate-pecan sundae sauce for a triple chocolate treat*

1½ c. sugar
1 tblsp. flour
¼ tsp. salt
2 c. milk
4 eggs, slightly beaten
3 squares unsweetened
  chocolate, melted

2 c. heavy cream
1 tblsp. vanilla
2 squares semisweet chocolate,
  chopped

Combine sugar, flour and salt. Gradually stir in milk. Add eggs. Cook, stirring constantly, until mixture thickens. Stir in melted chocolate. Cool.

Add cream and vanilla. Pour into 1-gal. freezer can. Freeze until mushy. Add chopped chocolate. Continue to freeze by basic directions (see "Freezing and Ripening Ice Cream" in Index). Makes about 1 gallon.

### CHOCOLATE ICE CREAM

*Top with marshmallow sauce and toasted angel flake coconut*

⅔ c. cocoa
2⅓ c. sugar
¼ tsp. salt
1 qt. milk

6 eggs, well beaten
3 c. heavy cream
1 tblsp. vanilla
Milk

Combine cocoa, sugar and salt in saucepan. Gradually stir in 1 qt. milk. Add eggs and cook over medium heat, stirring constantly. Bring mixture to a boil. Remove from heat and cool slightly.

Stir in cream and vanilla. Pour into 1-gal. freezer can and add enough milk to fill can two thirds full. Freeze by basic directions (see "Freezing and Ripening Ice Cream" in Index). Makes about 1 gallon.

## GERMAN CHOCOLATE ICE CREAM

*Scoop into sundae glasses and top with toasted coconut and pecans*

| | |
|---|---|
| 2 c. milk | 1½ c. sugar |
| 1 stick cinnamon | Dash of salt |
| 6 squares sweet cooking | 2 tblsp. vanilla |
| chocolate, grated | 1 qt. light cream |
| 3 eggs, separated | 2 c. milk |

Scald 2 c. milk, cinnamon and chocolate in top of double boiler over hot water.

Meanwhile, beat egg whites until frothy; gradually beat in ¾ c. sugar. Set aside.

Beat egg yolks, remaining ¾ c. sugar and salt together until light. Slowly stir egg yolk mixture into scalded milk. Cook, stirring constantly, until mixture coats spoon, about 5 minutes.

Remove from heat. Strain into 1-gal. freezer can. Add egg whites and mix well. Add vanilla, light cream and milk, filling freezer two thirds full. Mix well. Let cool, then freeze by basic directions (see "Freezing and Ripening Ice Cream" in Index). Makes 1 gallon.

## CHOCOLATE MINT ICE CREAM

*Sprinkle with crushed peppermint candy canes for holiday dessert*

| | |
|---|---|
| 2 c. sugar | 1 tsp. peppermint extract |
| ¼ c. flour | 1 tsp. green food color |
| ¼ tsp. salt | 3 c. heavy cream |
| 7 c. milk (about) | 4 squares semisweet chocolate, |
| 5 eggs | chopped |

Combine sugar, flour and salt. Stir in a little milk to make a thin paste.

Beat eggs; add sugar mixture, extract, food color and cream.

Pour into 1-gal. freezer can. Add milk to fill three fourths full. Freeze until mixture is slightly thickened. Add chocolate. Continue to freeze by basic directions (see "Freezing and Ripening Ice Cream" in Index). Makes 1 gallon.

## REFRESHING FRUIT MEDLEYS

"What flavor is this?" we asked as we dipped into a fruit-flaked ice cream. "Basic Vanilla with fruits I have on hand," a North Carolina farm wife answered. "When fresh fruits are in season I use a combination of them. In winter I use my home canned supply and then when I run out of that, it's fruit cocktail, cherries and bananas." Here are four of our most favorite combinations. Every one is a marvelous mixture of flavors.

### MIXED FRUIT ICE CREAM

*A good choice for making very special banana splits and sundaes*

5 eggs
1½ c. sugar
¼ tsp. salt
1 (14½ oz.) can evaporated milk
1 tblsp. vanilla
1 (10 oz.) pkg. frozen strawberries, thawed and drained

1 c. chopped canned peaches, drained
1 c. fruit cocktail, drained
1 (8½ oz.) can crushed pineapple, drained
3 bananas, mashed
2 c. light cream (about)

Beat eggs until lemon-colored. Gradually add sugar and salt. Add evaporated milk and vanilla; continue beating until well blended. Stir in strawberries, peaches, fruit cocktail, pineapple and bananas.

Pour into 1-gal. freezer can and add enough light cream to fill can two thirds full. Freeze by basic directions (see "Freezing and Ripening Ice Cream" in Index). Makes 1 gallon.

### THREE FRUIT MEDLEY

*Pass a plate of sugar-dusted gingerbread to serve with this*

1 (6 oz.) can frozen lemonade concentrate
1 (6 oz. can frozen orange juice concentrate
2 c. water
2 large bananas, mashed

2 c. sugar
1 c. heavy cream
3 c. milk
1 (1 lb. 14 oz.) can apricot halves, drained and chopped
¼ c. cut-up maraschino cherries

Mix together lemonade concentrate, orange juice concentrate, water, bananas, sugar, heavy cream and milk; beat well. Stir in apricots and cherries.

Pour into 1-gal. freezer can. Freeze by basic directions (see "Freezing and Ripening Ice Cream" in Index). Makes 1 gallon.

## FRUIT SURPRISE ICE CREAM

*A great accompaniment for moist wedges of chocolate chiffon cake*

| | |
|---|---|
| 3 c. milk | ¾ c. lemon juice |
| 3 c. heavy cream | 1 c. orange juice |
| 3 c. sugar | 3 bananas, mashed |

Combine milk, heavy cream and sugar. Pour into 1-gal. freezer can. Freeze until mushy.

Add lemon juice, orange juice and bananas. Continue to freeze by basic directions (See "Freezing and Ripening Ice Cream" in Index). Makes 1 gallon.

## FRUITED VELVET ICE CREAM

*A pretty ice cream with luscious fruit flavors—simple to make*

| | |
|---|---|
| 1½ qts. light cream | ½ c. chopped maraschino |
| 4 eggs, beaten | cherries |
| 1½ c. sugar | ½ c. chopped fresh strawberries |
| 1 tsp. vanilla | ¼ c. sugar |
| ½ c. chopped nuts | 2 tsp. fresh lemon juice |
| ½ c. diced banana | ½ tsp. salt |
| ½ c. drained diced pineapple (canned) | |

Combine cream, eggs and 1½ c. sugar. Cook over very low heat, stirring constantly, until mixture coats the back of a metal spoon. Cool quickly in refrigerator. Add vanilla. Pour into 1-gal. freezer can; fill two thirds full.

Combine nuts, fruits, ¼ c. sugar, lemon juice and salt. Let stand 5 minutes. Add to mixture in freezer can. Freeze by basic directions (see "Freezing and Ripening Ice Cream" in Index). Makes 1 gallon.

## SINGLE FRUIT ICE CREAMS

There's a fruit ice cream for every season. Start with Rhubarb Ice Cream when the first pink stalks arrive in springtime. Later, Peach Ice Cream is one of the most popular, especially if you can pluck your own sun-ripened peaches from the tree. Interesting ice creams can be made with canned and frozen fruits, too . . . smooth raspberry, mellow peach, chunky pineapple, golden apricot and jewel-red maraschino cherries mixed with pecans.

### RASPBERRY ICE CREAM

*Serve with pieces of chiffon cake for an afternoon or evening snack*

| | |
|---|---|
| 5 eggs | 1 tblsp. vanilla |
| 2 c. sugar | 2 (10 oz.) pkgs. frozen |
| ½ tsp. salt | raspberries, thawed |
| 1 qt. light cream | Milk |

Beat eggs until light. Gradually add sugar and salt. Add light cream, vanilla and raspberries. Pour into 1-gal. freezer can; add enough milk to fill can three fourths full. Freeze by basic directions (see "Freezing and Ripening Ice Cream" in Index). Makes 1 gallon.

### PEACH/PECAN ICE CREAM

*A luscious accompaniment for squares of plain yellow or white cake*

| | |
|---|---|
| 5 eggs | 2 tblsp. vanilla |
| 1 c. sugar | ½ tsp. salt |
| 3 c. milk | 2 c. chopped fresh peaches |
| 1 qt. heavy cream | ½ c. chopped pecans |

Beat eggs until light and fluffy. Gradually add sugar and continue beating until mixture is stiff. Stir in milk, cream, vanilla, salt, peaches and pecans; mix thoroughly.

Pour into 1-gal. freezer can and freeze by basic directions (see "Freezing and Ripening Ice Cream" in Index). Makes 1 gallon.

## PINEAPPLE ICE CREAM

*This creamy smooth ice cream is studded with pineapple nuggets*

1 qt. milk
4 c. sugar
2 (8½ oz.) cans crushed
  pineapple, drained

¾ c. lemon juice
1⅔ c. orange juice
1 qt. milk
2 c. heavy cream

Scald 1 qt. milk. Add sugar and mix. Cool.

Add pineapple, lemon and orange juice to cooled milk; mix well. Stir in 1 qt. milk and heavy cream.

Freeze by basic directions (see "Freezing and Ripening Ice Cream" in Index). Makes about 1 gallon.

## APRICOT ICE CREAM

*A perfect go-with for lemon pound cake and steaming cups of tea*

2 c. heavy cream
2 c. dairy half-and-half
2 c. sugar
2 (1 lb. 14 oz.) cans pitted
  apricots, drained and chopped
  (1 qt.)

⅛ tsp. salt
1 tblsp. vanilla
Milk

Combine heavy cream, dairy half-and-half, sugar, apricots, salt and vanilla; blend well. Pour into 1-gal. freezer can. Add enough milk to fill can two thirds full.

Freeze by basic directions (see "Freezing and Ripening Ice Cream" in Index). Makes about 1 gallon.

## CHERRY/PECAN ICE CREAM

*Alternate layers of this ice cream with hot fudge sauce in tall stemmed parfait glasses and top with toasted pecans*

5 eggs
¾ c. sugar
¾ c. light corn syrup
1 (15 oz.) can sweetened
  condensed milk (not
  evaporated)

2 tblsp. lemon juice
1 tsp. vanilla
1 c. diced maraschino cherries,
  drained
¾ c. chopped pecans
Milk

Beat eggs. Add sugar, corn syrup, sweetened condensed milk, lemon juice and vanilla; blend well. Add cherries and nuts.

Pour into 1-gal. freezer can. Add enough milk to fill can three fourths full. Freeze by basic directions (see "Freezing and Ripening Ice Cream" in Index). Makes about 1 gallon.

## RHUBARB ICE CREAM

*Serve in pretty green glass dishes . . . looks and tastes like spring*

| | |
|---|---|
| 6 c. diced fresh rhubarb | 4 c. heavy cream |
| 1½ c. sugar | 1 tsp. vanilla |
| 2 c. water | ¼ tsp. red food color |
| ¼ c. lemon juice | 3 c. milk |
| ½ tsp. salt | |

Combine rhubarb, sugar, water, lemon juice and salt in 2-qt. saucepan. Cook, uncovered, 10 minutes, or until rhubarb is tender. Cool well.

Combine cooled rhubarb mixture, heavy cream, vanilla and red food color. Pour into 1-gal. freezer can. Add milk, filling two thirds full. Freeze by basic directions (see "Freezing and Ripening Ice Cream" in Index). Makes 1 gallon.

## GOLDEN GLOW ICE CREAM

*Use egg yolks left after baking angel cake in this great dessert*

| | |
|---|---|
| ¼ c. grated orange peel | ½ tsp. salt |
| 2 c. milk | 8 egg yolks, beaten |
| 1 c. sugar | 2 c. light cream |
| 1 c. light corn syrup | 4 c. fresh orange juice |

Place orange peel in small cheesecloth bag. Scald with milk in top of double boiler.

Add sugar, corn syrup and salt to egg yolks, which have been mixed with some hot milk.

Cook, stirring constantly, until mixture coats spoon; cool.

Stir in cream and orange juice. Pour into 1-gal. freezer can. Freeze by basic directions (see "Freezing and Ripening Ice Cream" in Index). Makes 1 gallon.

# STRAWBERRY FOR ME, PLEASE

Strawberry is the very first choice of all the fruit flavors. And there's nothing that tastes fresher or brigher than homemade strawberry ice cream made with fat juicy berries. We feature recipes with frozen berries, too, so you can enjoy this popular flavor year round.

## STRAWBERRY ICE CREAM

*Garnish with a dollop of whipped cream and a luscious strawberry*

2 (3 oz.) pkgs. strawberry flavor
  gelatin
1½ c. sugar
2 c. boiling water
4 eggs, well beaten

1 qt. milk
2 c. heavy cream
2 tsp. vanilla
1 (10 oz.) pkg. frozen
  strawberries, thawed

Dissolve gelatin and sugar in boiling water. Add eggs, milk, cream and vanilla. Stir until well blended. Stir in strawberries.

Pour into 1-gal. freezer can and freeze by basic directions (see "Freezing and Ripening Ice Cream" in Index). Makes 1 gallon.

## STRAWBERRY/BANANA ICE CREAM

*A combination of two favorite fruit flavors—great for sundaes*

4 eggs
1 c. sugar
4 c. heavy cream
1 tblsp. vanilla
¼ tsp. salt
2 (10 oz.) pkgs. frozen
  strawberries, thawed and
  drained

6 bananas, mashed
1 c. walnuts
Milk

Beat eggs until light and fluffy. Gradually add sugar; beat until mixture becomes thick. Add heavy cream, vanilla, salt, strawberries, bananas and nuts; mix well.

Pour into 1-gal. freezer can and add enough milk to fill can two thirds full. Freeze by basic directions (see "Freezing and Ripening Ice Cream" in Index). Makes 1 gallon.

## STRAWBERRY FROST

*Cross between an ice cream and a sherbet—refreshing dessert*

| | |
|---|---|
| 1 qt. strawberries (about) | 1 envelope unflavored gelatin |
| ¼ c. unsweetened applesauce | ¼ c. cold water |
| 1 c. sugar | ¾ c. boiling water |

Put strawberries through food mill or electric blender to make purée (you should have 1¾ c.). Add applesauce and sugar.

Soften gelatin in cold water. Dissolve in boiling water; add to fruit mixture and blend. Pour into 2-qt. freezer can.

Freeze by basic directions (see "Freezing and Ripening Ice Cream" in Index). Or pour mixture into 2 refrigerator trays and partially freeze. Spoon it into large bowl and beat until light and fluffy. Work quickly so that frost will not melt. Return to refrigerator trays and freeze until firm. Makes 1½ quarts.

## *Variations*

**Raspberry Frost:** Use 1¼ c. raspberry purée and ¾ c. applesauce.

**Blackberry Frost:** Use 1¼ c. blackberry purée and ¾ c. applesauce.

**Blueberry Frost:** Use 1½ c. blueberry purée and ½ c. applesauce. Add 1 tsp. lemon juice.

**Elderberry Frost:** Use 1½ c. elderberry purée and ½ c. applesauce.

**Cherry Frost:** Use 1¼ c. cherry purée and ¾ c. applesauce.

**Cranberry Frost:** Use 1½ c. canned strained cranberry sauce, ½ c. applesauce and ½ c. sugar.

**Rhubarb Frost:** Use 1½ c. sweetened rhubarb sauce and ½ c. applesauce.

**Peach Frost:** Use 1¾ c. peach purée and ¼ c. applesauce.

# WINTER SPECIALS

Spicy pumpkin ice cream will make a big hit with the Halloween goblins. As the grande finale to Thanksgiving, why not offer homemade Pumpkin Ice Cream rolled in chopped nuts. Pass a pitcher of warmed maple syrup for those who are partial to sundaes.

Pink Peppermint Ice Cream is perfect for Christmas treats. Make several batches ahead and store in your freezer. When friends drop in, dish up the ice cream and add a sprinkling of crushed peppermint candy for a gala dessert.

## PUMPKIN ICE CREAM

*Scoop into baked tart shells for a special Thanksgiving dessert*

| | |
|---|---|
| 2 c. milk | 1 tsp. ground nutmeg |
| 4 egg yolks | ½ tsp. ground allspice |
| ⅔ c. sugar | ¼ tsp. ground ginger |
| ⅛ tsp. salt | 1 c. heavy cream |
| 2 c. cooked or canned pumpkin | ½ tsp. vanilla |
| 2 tsp. ground cinnamon | |

Scald milk in double boiler.

Beat egg yolks well; combine with sugar. Add salt, pumpkin and spices. Combine with milk in double boiler and cook 4 minutes. Add cream and vanilla.

Pour into 1-gal. freezer can. Freeze by basic directions (see "Freezing and Ripening Ice Cream" in Index). Makes about 2 quarts.

## PEPPERMINT ICE CREAM

*A peppermint-flavored ice cream which is perfect for the holidays*

| | |
|---|---|
| 2 c. milk | 2 c. heavy cream |
| 2 eggs | 8 drops peppermint extract |
| 1 c. sugar | 24 drops green food color |
| ½ c. light corn syrup | |

Scald milk in top of double boiler.

Beat eggs, sugar and corn syrup together with rotary beater. Add to hot milk, stirring constantly. Cook over boiling water 5 minutes, or until of custard consistency. Remove from heat. Stir in cream, peppermint extract and food color. Cool well.

Pour into 1-gal. freezer can. Freeze by basic directions (see "Freezing and Ripening Ice Cream" in Index). Makes 1½ quarts.

## ROCKY ROAD ICE CREAM

*A scrumptious combination of all the ingredients children like*

2 tblsp. unflavored gelatin
3 c. milk
2 c. sugar
¼ tsp. salt
6 eggs
1½ qts. light cream
1 (3¾ oz.) pkg. vanilla instant
  pudding

3 tblsp. vanilla
2 c. miniature marshmallows
4 squares semisweet chocolate,
  chopped
1 c. broken-up peanut brittle

Soften gelatin in ½ c. cold milk. Scald 1½ c. milk. Add scalded milk to gelatin mixture, stirring well. Add sugar and salt.

Beat eggs well (about 5 minutes). Beat in gelatin mixture, cream, pudding mix, vanilla and remaining 1 c. milk.

Pour into 1-gal. freezer can. Freeze until mixture begins to thicken. Remove dasher; add marshmallows, chocolate and peanut brittle. Continue to freeze by basic directions (see "Freezing and Ripening Ice Cream" in Index). Makes 1 gallon.

## COFFEE/WALNUT ICE CREAM

*Tastes wonderful by itself or with toasted pound cake fingers*

4 tsp. instant coffee
2½ c. sugar
2 tblsp. flour
¼ tsp. salt
2½ c. milk

2½ c. cold coffee
6 egg yolks, slightly beaten
5 c. heavy cream
2 tblsp. vanilla
2 c. chopped walnuts

Combine coffee, sugar, flour and salt in large saucepan. Gradually stir in milk and coffee. Cook, stirring constantly, until mixture is slightly thickened. Pour some of the hot mixture over the eggs, blending well. Slowly stir egg mixture into hot mixture. Cook 1 minute. Chill well.

Combine chilled coffee mixture, heavy cream, vanilla and walnuts. Pour into 1-gal. freezer can. Freeze by basic directions (see "Freezing and Ripening Ice Cream" in Index). Makes 1 gallon.

## CARAMEL ICE CREAM

*Add crunchiness by topping with small pieces of peanut brittle*

| | |
|---|---|
| 1½ c. sugar | ¾ tsp. salt |
| 2¼ c. boiling water | 3 (14½ oz.) cans evaporated |
| 6 eggs | milk |
| ¾ c. sugar | 1 tblsp. vanilla |

Melt 1½ c. sugar in heavy skillet over low heat until golden brown. Remove from heat; slowly stir in boiling water; cool.

Beat eggs until light, adding ¾ c. sugar and salt. Stir in caramel syrup, evaporated milk and vanilla. Pour into 1-gal. freezer can and freeze by basic directions (see "Freezing and Ripening Ice Cream" in Index). Makes about 1 gallon.

## COCONUT/HONEY ICE CREAM

*For a tropical flavor try this with orange blossom honey*

| | |
|---|---|
| 1½ c. honey | ½ tsp. salt |
| 4 eggs, slightly beaten | 3 c. milk |
| 3 c. heavy cream | 1 (3½ oz.) can flaked coconut |
| 2 tsp. vanilla | 2 (8½ oz.) cans crushed |
| ½ tsp. lemon extract | pineapple |

Add honey to eggs; mix well. Add cream, flavorings, salt and milk; stir until well blended. Chill.

Pour into 1-gal. freezer can; freeze by basic directions (see "Freezing and Ripening Ice Cream" in Index).

When partly frozen, add coconut and pineapple; continue freezing until crank turns hard. Remove dasher and let ripen. Or spoon into freezer containers, and store in freezer. Makes 1 gallon.

NOTE: To intensify coconut flavor, add 2 tsp. coconut extract with lemon extract and vanilla.

# EXOTIC ICE CREAMS

Dazzle your guests with either one of these two very different flavored ice creams. Orange Pekoe Tea Ice Cream, with its delicate undertone of orange flavor could be the hit of the party.

Snowy-white Rice Ice Cream would be the perfect ending to a Chinese dinner. Ask your guests to "guess the flavor." For an effective summer dessert, spoon ice cream into plain glass dishes and use a large green leaf as an underliner.

## ORANGE PEKOE TEA ICE CREAM

*A refreshing ice cream made with a tea base and a hint of orange*

| | |
|---|---|
| 2½ c. milk, scalded | ¼ tsp. salt |
| 6 whole cloves | ¾ c. sugar |
| 1 tblsp. grated orange peel | 4 egg yolks, slightly beaten |
| 2 tblsp. orange pekoe tea | ¾ c. honey |
| 1 envelope unflavored gelatin | 3 c. light cream |
| ⅓ c. cold water | 4 egg whites, stiffly beaten |

Scald milk with cloves and orange peel. Add tea; let stand 5 to 8 minutes over hot water.

Soften gelatin in water.

Strain milk; return to double boiler top. Add salt, sugar and egg yolks, which have been mixed with some hot milk. Cook, stirring constantly, until thickened.

Remove from heat, add softened gelatin; blend thoroughly. Add honey. Cool.

When cold, stir in cream and fold in egg whites. Pour into 1-gal. freezer can. Freeze by basic directions (see "Freezing and Ripening Ice Cream" in Index). Makes 1 gallon.

## RICE ICE CREAM

*Pineapple and rice make this an interesting and different ice cream*

| | |
|---|---|
| 1½ c. cooked rice | ⅛ tsp. salt |
| 2 c. milk | 1 qt. milk |
| 1 c. heavy cream | 1 (1 lb. 4 oz.) can crushed |
| 4 eggs, well beaten | pineapple |
| 2 (15 oz.) cans sweetened condensed milk (not evaporated) | ¼ c. lemon juice |

Mash the rice while hot with a fork. Place in saucepan with 2 c. milk and cream.

Add eggs to hot rice mixture. Cook about 1 minute, stirring constantly. Add sweetened condensed milk and salt. Stir well.

Pour into 1-gal. freezer can. Stir in 1 qt. milk, or as much as needed to make the freezer three fourths full. Freeze until mushy.

Add pineapple and lemon juice. Continue freezing by basic directions (see "Freezing and Ripening Ice Cream" in Index). Makes 1 gallon.

NOTE: To freeze in refrigerator trays, make only one half of recipe. When mixture is mushy, turn into chilled bowl and beat thoroughly; stir in pineapple and lemon juice. Return to refrigerator trays and freeze until firm.

## SUMMER SHERBETS

Next time you're asked to bring homemade ice cream to a neighborhood picnic, why not make a gallon of cool refreshing sherbet. Take your choice of Strawberry, Creamy Lime, Rhubarb Cream or Cantaloupe Melbet.

### FRESH STRAWBERRY SHERBET

*Pretty, coral-red dessert to make when the strawberries are ripe*

| | |
|---|---|
| 4 qts. fresh strawberries, sliced | ⅔ c. orange juice |
| 4 c. sugar | ⅛ tsp. ground cinnamon |
| 2⅔ c. milk | |

Mix strawberries and sugar; let stand until juicy (about 1½ hours). Mash, or purée in blender. Strain out seeds (optional, but we prefer seedless sherbet).

Add milk, orange juice and cinnamon. Mix well. Pour into 1-gal. freezer can. Freeze by basic directions (see "Freezing and Ripening Ice Cream" in Index). (Or pour mixture into refrigerator trays or loaf pans; freeze about 3 hours; stir 2 or 3 times.) Makes about 1 gallon.

### *Variations*

**Strawberry Parfait Ring:** Spoon strawberry sherbet and soft vanilla ice cream in alternating layers in chilled ring mold. Freeze. When frozen, unmold on serving plate; return to freezer. To serve, fill center with fresh berries for color-bright garnish.

**Strawberry/Lemon Parfait:** Spoon strawberry and lemon sherbets alternately into parfait glasses or tumblers. Return to freezer until time to serve. Garnish with fresh berries.

**Chocolate/Strawberry Ring:** Spoon sherbet into ring mold. Freeze. When frozen, unmold on plate; return to freezer. To serve, fill center with scoops of chocolate ice cream.

**Water Sherbet:** Use water instead of milk. Sherbet is smoother and tastes better when made with milk however.

## CREAMY LIME SHERBET

*Garnish each serving with two bright red strawberry halves*

| | |
|---|---|
| 1 (3 oz.) pkg. lime flavor gelatin | 1 (6 oz.) can frozen limeade concentrate |
| 1 c. boiling water | 8 drops green food color |
| 1¼ c. sugar | 4 c. milk |
| ⅛ tsp. salt | 2 c. light cream |

Dissolve gelatin in boiling water. Add sugar and salt. Add limeade, stirring until thawed. Stir in food color, milk and light cream.

Pour into 1-gal. freezer can. Freeze by basic directions (see "Freezing and Ripening Ice Cream" in Index). Makes 1 gallon.

## RHUBARB CREAM SHERBET

*Cool and creamy with just the right nip of tartness to end a meal*

| | |
|---|---|
| 2½ c. finely diced rhubarb | ¼ tsp. salt |
| 2 c. sugar | 2 eggs |
| 2 tblsp. lemon juice | 2 c. milk |
| ½ c. light corn syrup | 1 c. heavy cream |

Put rhubarb and sugar in saucepan. Bring to a boil—then simmer 5 minutes, until tender. Remove from heat. Stir in lemon juice, corn syrup and salt. Let cool.

Beat eggs; add milk and cream. Pour mixture into 2-qt. freezer can; pack with ice and salt (see "Freezing and Ripening Ice

Cream" in Index). When freezer is all packed, add rhubarb mixture. Freeze by basic directions. Makes 2 quarts.

## CANTALOUPE MELBET

*Lovely to look at, luscious to eat—serve it when you want to splurge*

| | |
|---|---|
| 3 c. cantaloupe purée (1 | ⅛ tsp. salt |
| cantaloupe) | 1 envelope unflavored gelatin |
| ¾ c. sugar | ¼ c. cool water |
| 1 tblsp. lemon juice | |

Use ripe, sound cantaloupe; cut in half. Remove seeds and peel. Slice and press through a food mill or sieve to make purée. Or use electric blender.

Mix cantaloupe purée, sugar, lemon juice and salt. Soften gelatin in cool water 5 minutes; then dissolve by heating over boiling water. Add cantaloupe mixture slowly to gelatin, stirring while adding to mix thoroughly.

*For electric ice-cream freezer,* pour into 2-qt. freezer container and freeze by basic directions (see "Freezing and Ripening Ice Cream" in Index). Serve immediately, do not let ripen. Makes about 1 quart.

*For refrigerator trays,* pour mixture into trays, and freeze until firm. Remove trays and stir rapidly to incorporate air and make it smoother. Return trays to freezer a few hours to harden. Serve immediately or pack in freezer containers and store in freezer. It will keep up to 3 weeks.

# CHAPTER 3

# Refrigerator Tray
# Ice Creams and Sherbets

When you're in the mood for ice cream and don't have time to turn a freezer, make it in refrigerator trays. It might not be *quite* as good as the homemade churned cream but a refreshing treat nonetheless and preferred to the commercial products, many farm families tell us.

We selected some imaginative ice cream recipes that can be stirred together, poured into the refrigerator tray, and then popped into the freezing section until you are ready to serve them. You'll want to make the basic Vanilla, and then try the coffee that has an instant pudding base—and on and on.

Many farm families like an icy sherbet on a sultry day. In the cool of the morning mix up a lemon or orange or fruit medley sherbet for a supper treat. Everyone will take seconds!

You'll love our Grapefruit Sherbet made with heavy cream. The Cranberry Sherbet looks and tastes marvelous nestled in a wedge of honeydew melon. One farm homemaker surprises her guests with an appetizer of Ruby Red Cranberry Sherbet in a scooped out lemon shell—it looks dramatic and is easy to fix and freeze ahead. Avocado Sherbet, smooth and mellow flavored, tastes wonderful as topping for a fresh fruit salad.

## VANILLA ICE CREAM

*Rich, creamy and oh-so-good . . . be sure to try the three variations*

| | |
|---|---|
| 6 eggs | 2 tsp. vanilla |
| 1 c. sugar | ½ tsp. salt |
| 2 c. milk | 2 c. heavy cream, whipped |

Beat eggs until thick and lemon colored.

Add sugar, milk, vanilla and salt; blend well. Fold into whipped cream. Pour into 2 cold refrigerator trays. Freeze until partially set.

Break into chunks in large, chilled bowl. Beat until light and fluffy, but not melted.

Return to trays; freeze until firm. "Mellow" it in the refrigerator section about 30 minutes before serving. Makes 8 servings.

## Variations

**Maple Nut:** Substitute 2 tsp. maple flavoring for vanilla; add ½ c. hickory nuts or pecans at second beating.

**Strawberry Ice Cream:** Slice 2 c. fresh strawberries; sprinkle with ¼ c. sugar. Let stand while you make ice cream; omit vanilla. Add berries at second beating. (Mixer will chop up berries.)

**Peppermint Ice Cream:** Omit vanilla from basic ice cream recipe; decrease sugar to ½ c. Freeze partially. Beat in well ⅔ c. crushed peppermint candies. Measure out 1½ c. of the ice cream, add ⅛ tsp. red food color. Pour remaining ice cream in 9″ square pan. Drizzle pink ice cream over plain, swirl with spatula. Freeze. Serve on squares of chocolate cake, baked from prepared mix.

**Sherbets:** Prepare basic recipe, decreasing milk to 1 c. At second beating: for orange, add 1 (6 oz.) can frozen orange juice concentrate, partially thawed; for raspberry, add 1 c. red raspberry purée; for lime, add 1 c. water, 1 tsp. lime extract, and ¼ tsp. green food color.


### VANILLA ICE CREAM

*Have a make-your-own-sundae party: Guests help themselves to assorted sauces, chopped nuts, coconut and whipped cream*

| | |
|---|---|
| ½ c. sugar | 2 c. milk |
| 2 tblsp. cornstarch | 1½ tsp. vanilla |
| ½ tsp. salt | 1 c. heavy cream, whipped |
| 1 egg | |

Mix sugar, cornstarch and salt in top of double boiler. Add egg and mix well. Gradually add milk. Place over boiling water and cook, stirring constantly, until mixture is slightly thickened, about 5 to 6 minutes. Remove from heat, add vanilla; cool. Pour into refrigerator tray; freeze until just firm.

Remove chilled mixture to bowl; beat with rotary beater. Fold in whipped cream; blend well. Return to refrigerator tray; freeze 2 to 3 hours. Makes about 1 quart.

NOTE: You can substitute 1 c. evaporated milk, chilled and whipped for the heavy cream.

## Variations

**Chocolate Ice Cream:** Omit egg and add 2 squares unsweetened chocolate to mixture before cooking.

**Coffee Ice Cream:** Omit vanilla. Substitute 1 cup strong coffee for 1 cup of milk.

### COFFEE ICE CREAM

*Satiny-smooth ice cream that's easy to make—do try the variations*

1 c. evaporated milk
½ c. heavy cream
¼ c. sugar
2 tsp. unflavored gelatin
2 tblsp. instant coffee
⅛ tsp. salt

½ c. hot milk
1 (3¾ oz.) pkg. vanilla instant pudding
2 c. cold milk
½ tsp. vanilla

Pour evaporated milk into a refrigerator tray. Chill in freezer until fine crystals begin to form around edges.

Chill cream, bowl and beaters.

Combine sugar, gelatin, instant coffee and salt; mix well. Gradually add hot milk, stirring until mixture is smooth.

Mix instant pudding according to package directions, using the 2 c. milk. Add coffee mixture and vanilla.

Combine chilled evaporated milk and heavy cream in chilled bowl; beat until mixture forms soft peaks. Fold in pudding mixture. Pour into 2 refrigerator trays; freeze until firm around edges.

Remove partially frozen mixture to chilled bowl; beat with a spoon until smooth. Return to refrigerator trays and freeze until firm. Makes 1½ quarts.

## Variations

Follow directions for Coffee Ice Cream, but omit the instant coffee, and add ingredients as indicated:

**Banana Ice Cream:** Beat or mash until smooth, 3 ripe medium bananas. Stir in 1 tblsp. lemon juice. Add to combined pudding and gelatin mixture.

**Chocolate Ice Cream:** Use chocolate instead of vanilla pudding. Add ¼ c. cocoa to sugar-gelatin mixture.

**Butterscotch/Nut Ice Cream:** Use butterscotch instead of vanilla pudding. Add ½ c. chopped pecans or walnuts to mixture before putting in tray to freeze.

# LIGHT AND LEMONY

End the meal on a refreshing note by serving lemon sherbet or ice cream. Choose either our smooth Lemon Ice Cream, Lemon/Apricot Ice Cream, a delightful blend of flavors, or Lemonade Ice Cream—you'll want to make all three often.

## LEMON ICE CREAM

*Garnish with whole berries or fruit slices of contrasting colors*

| | |
|---|---|
| 3 eggs, separated | 1 (4 oz.) pkg. marshmallows (16) |
| 1 c. milk | 1½ tsp. grated lemon peel |
| ¾ c. sugar | ½ c. lemon juice |
| ⅛ tsp. salt | 1 c. heavy cream |

Combine egg yolks, milk, sugar and salt in top of double boiler; beat slightly. Cook over boiling water, stirring constantly, until mixture thickens slightly and coats a metal spoon. Remove from heat.

Add marshmallows. Stir until coated with custard mixture. Cover and let stand 10 minutes, then blend in softened marshmallows. Add lemon peel and juice.

Beat egg whites until stiff. Fold into custard mixture. Pour into 2 refrigerator trays. Freeze until mushy.

Whip cream until stiff.

Turn custard mixture into chilled bowl. Beat with rotary beater just until smooth; do not let mixture melt. Fold in whipped cream. Return to refrigerator trays and freeze until firm; stir once or twice during freezing. Makes 1 quart.

## Variations

Follow directions for Lemon Ice Cream, but omit lemon peel and juice; add ingredients as indicated:

**Lime Ice Cream:** Add 1½ tsp. grated lime peel, ⅓ c. lime juice and 4 drops green food color to custard base.

**Orange/Pineapple Ice Cream:** Add 1 tblsp. grated orange peel, ½ c. orange juice and 1 (8¼ oz.) can crushed pineapple, drained, to custard base.

**Strawberry Ice Cream:** Add 1¼ c. crushed fresh strawberries—or 1 package (10 to 12½ oz.) frozen berries, thawed—and 2 tblsp. lemon juice to custard base. (Reduce sugar to ½ c. if you use sweetened berries.)

**Peach Ice Cream:** Add 1¼ c. mashed ripe peaches, or 1 (10 oz.) pkg. frozen peaches, thawed and mashed, and 2 tblsp. lemon juice to custard base. (Reduce sugar to ½ c. if you use sweetened frozen peaches.)

## LEMON/APRICOT ICE CREAM

*A wonderful year-around dessert for special occasions and parties*

| | |
|---|---|
| 2 (6 oz.) cans evaporated milk | ¼ c. light corn syrup |
| 1 (3¾ oz.) pkg. lemon instant pudding | 1 tblsp. lemon juice |
| | 2 tsp. grated lemon peel |
| 1 (14½ oz.) can evaporated milk | 1 (6 oz.) can frozen lemonade |
| 3 (7¾ oz.) jars strained apricot/apple baby food | concentrate, thawed |

Empty each small can of milk into a separate refrigerator tray. Chill until fine crystals form around edges. (If milk freezes more, thaw until there are only a few ice crystals.)

Prepare pudding according to package directions using only the 14½-ounce can of evaporated milk for liquid.

When pudding is set, add ½ cup of it to apricot/apple baby food and corn syrup.

Turn milk from one refrigerator tray into chilled bowl; whip quickly until very stiff. Add lemon juice and blend. (If whipped milk begins to fall, return to refrigerator tray and rechill.)

Fold into apricot mixture. (If desired, add food color. For apricot, mix ½ tsp. red and 1 tsp. yellow.) Pour into two 9×5×3″ loaf pans. Freeze while fixing second layer.

Add lemon peel and lemonade concentrate to remaining pudding mixture.

Whip milk from second tray. Fold into lemon mixture. Pour over apricot layers in pans. Freeze until firm. Slice to serve. Makes 2½ quarts.

## LEMONADE ICE CREAM

*A tangy ice cream that can be whipped up on an extra busy day*

3 envelopes dessert topping mix     3 egg whites, stiffly beaten
½ c. sugar
1 (6 oz.) can frozen lemonade
   concentrate

Prepare dessert topping mix by package directions. Add sugar and frozen lemonade concentrate. Fold in egg whites.

Pour into refrigerator trays or loaf pans; cover and freeze until firm. Makes 2 quarts.

## ORANGE/COCONUT VELVET

*Team with wedges of soft angel cake for applause-winning dessert*

1 c. orange juice          ¾ c. evaporated milk
½ c. sugar                 1 tblsp. lemon juice
⅛ tsp. salt                ¼ c. chopped shredded coconut

Mix orange juice, sugar, and salt. Freeze to a mush in refrigerator tray.

Chill evaporated milk in refrigerator tray for 1 hour, then whip. Add lemon juice; whip until stiff.

Fold orange mush and coconut into whipped milk. Return to refrigerator tray. Freeze until firm. Makes 4 servings.

## REFRIGERATOR MINT ICE CREAM

*For a refreshing sundae—top with hot fudge sauce and nuts*

| | |
|---|---|
| 1 tsp. unflavored gelatin | 3 tblsp. sugar |
| 2 tblsp. cold water | 1 egg, separated |
| 1 c. scalded milk | 1 c. heavy cream, whipped |
| 1 tsp. flour | ½ tsp. peppermint extract |
| ⅛ tsp. salt | 4 to 6 drops green food color |

Soften gelatin in cold water; dissolve in hot milk.

Mix flour, salt and sugar; add to milk mixture; cook until thickened.

Cover; cook 10 minutes over hot water. Slowly add mixture to slightly beaten egg yolk; return to double boiler and cook 1 minute longer. Strain into refrigerator tray; chill.

Pour into chilled bowl; beat until light. Fold in whipped cream and stiffly beaten egg white; blend in peppermint extract and food color.

Pour into refrigerator tray and freeze. Makes about 1 quart.

# VERSATILE FRUIT SHERBETS

It's easy to stir up a refrigerator tray sherbet to fit into a variety of menu roles. Start your meal on a tangy note, for instance—spoon a fruit sherbet into the center of a fruit cup. For a light refreshing summer fruit salad, add a surprise scoop of Apple Spice Sherbet to a Waldorf salad just before serving. Serve tart Cranberry Sherbet in tiny paper cups as an accompaniment to chicken salad. For dessert, arrange fresh orange sections in a sherbet glass and spoon on a dollop of Grapefruit Sherbet. Or try a dish of sliced bananas topped with Peach Sherbet for a light dessert. Spoon honeydew melon cubes or balls over a helping of homemade Pineapple Sherbet or present a double strawberry treat, Surprise Strawberry Sherbet with bright fresh strawberries.

## APPLE SPICE SHERBET

*This spicy apple sherbet is perfect on wedges of warm apple pie*

| | |
|---|---|
| 2 c. applesauce | Dash of ground nutmeg |
| ¾ c. confectioners sugar | 1 tsp. vanilla |
| ¼ tsp. salt | 2 egg whites |
| ⅛ tsp. ground cinnamon | 2 tblsp. lemon juice |

Place applesauce, sugar, salt, cinnamon, nutmeg, vanilla, egg whites and lemon juice in large bowl of electric mixer. Beat at high speed until firm peaks form, about 5 minutes. Spoon into 9″ square pan. Freeze until firm, about 2 hours. Makes 6 to 8 servings.

## CRANBERRY SHERBET

*Serve this colorful cranberry sherbet with Christmas cookies*

| | |
|---|---|
| 1 envelope unflavored gelatin | ½ c. orange juice |
| 1 c. sugar | 1 tsp. orange peel |
| ¼ c. cold water | 2 egg whites |
| ½ c. water | ⅛ tsp. salt |
| 2 c. cranberry juice cocktail | |

Soften gelatin in cold water. Combine sugar and water in saucepan; bring to boil and boil 5 minutes. Dissolve gelatin in hot syrup; cool. Add cranberry juice cocktail, orange juice and peel. Pour into refrigerator tray and freeze until it begins to set around the edges. Remove to chilled bowl and beat until fluffy, but not enough to melt.

Beat egg whites and salt until stiff but not dry; fold into cranberry mixture. Return mixture to refrigerator tray and freeze until firm, about 4 hours, stirring occasionally from back to front of tray. Makes 6 servings.

## RUBY RED CRANBERRY SHERBET

*A delicious accompaniment for cold sliced turkey and pork roast*

4 c. cranberries (about 1 lb.)
½ c. water
½ c. sugar
¾ c. water
1 envelope unflavored gelatin

¼ c. cold water
½ c. lemon juice
2 c. sugar
1 c. heavy cream

Cook cranberries in ½ c. water until skins pop. Put cranberries through food mill.

Combine ½ c. sugar and ¾ c. water; boil 5 minutes.

Soften gelatin in ¼ c. cold water. Add to hot sugar syrup and stir until gelatin dissolves.

Add lemon juice and 2 c. sugar to cranberry pulp. Combine with syrup.

Cool. Add cream (do not whip); freeze in 8½×4½×2½" loaf pan until mushy, then beat. Return to freezer and freeze until firm. Store tightly covered. Makes about 1 quart.

## GRAPEFRUIT SHERBET

*Drop scoopfuls of this tangy sherbet into your favorite fruit punch*

1½ c. canned or fresh grapefruit
juice
¾ c. sugar
¾ c. orange juice
2 tsp. grated orange peel

1 egg, separated
1 c. heavy cream
⅛ tsp. salt
¼ c. sugar

Combine grapefruit juice and ¾ c. sugar in saucepan. Heat; stir to dissolve sugar. Remove from heat; add orange juice and peel. Pour into refrigerator trays and chill in freezer until mushy.

Beat egg yolk until light colored.

Whip cream; add salt, ¼ c. sugar and beaten egg yolk. Mix well.

Beat egg white until stiff. Fold into cream mixture.

Remove partially frozen fruit mixture and stir into cream. Return to trays and freeze until sherbet is frozen ¼" around sides of trays, about 30 minutes. Remove from trays and stir thoroughly. Freeze. Makes 8 to 10 servings.

## FRUIT SHERBET

*Choose your family's favorite fruit and whip it into a sherbet*

| | |
|---|---|
| 1 c. mashed strawberries, pineapple, peaches, pears, or other fruit | Juice of 1 lemon |
| | Juice of 1 orange |
| | 1 c. sugar |
| 1 mashed ripe banana | 1 c. light cream |

Beat all ingredients together until thoroughly blended. Pour into refrigerator tray and freeze 1 hour.

Remove sherbet from freezing compartment and stir. Freeze 1 hour longer, or until firm. Makes 6 servings.

## PEACH SHERBET

*Serve mixed fruit salad topped with peach sherbet for dessert*

| | |
|---|---|
| 1 c. milk | ⅓ c. lemon juice |
| ¾ c. light corn syrup | 2 egg whites, stiffly beaten |
| 1 c. sugar | |
| 2 (10 oz.) pkgs. frozen peaches, thawed | |

Scald milk with corn syrup and sugar over low heat. Stir until sugar is dissolved. Cool.

Meanwhile, put peaches in blender and blend well; you should have 2 c. peach pulp and juice. Add peach pulp and lemon juice to cooled mixture. Pour into refrigerator trays and freeze until firm.

Remove sherbet to chilled bowl; break up with wooden spoon and beat until free from hard lumps but still a thick mush. Fold in egg whites. Return to refrigerator trays and freeze until firm. Makes about 8 servings.

## PINEAPPLE SHERBET

*Pineapple sherbet is great to serve even after the heartiest meal*

| | |
|---|---|
| ¾ c. sugar | 2 tblsp. lemon juice |
| ⅓ c. water | 1 c. light cream |
| 1½ c. pineapple juice | 2 egg whites, stiffly beaten |
| 1 (8¼ oz.) can crushed pineapple, drained | |

Combine sugar, water and pineapple juice in saucepan; cook 15 minutes. Remove from heat; add crushed pineapple and lemon juice. Cool. Pour into refrigerator tray and freeze until mushy.

Remove partially frozen mixture to chilled bowl; beat until light, gradually adding cream. Beat well. Fold in egg whites. Return to refrigerator tray and freeze until firm. Makes about 6 servings.

## SURPRISE STRAWBERRY SHERBET

*Angel food cake is an ideal companion for this pretty pink sherbet*

| | |
|---|---|
| 1 pt. fresh strawberries, sliced | 1½ c. buttermilk |
| ¼ c. sugar | ½ c. sugar |
| 1 envelope unflavored gelatin | 2 tblsp. lemon juice |
| ⅓ c. strawberry juice | |

Combine strawberries and the ¼ c. sugar and mash well. Let stand 10 minutes then strain off ⅓ c. juice. Set aside remaining crushed berries.

Soften gelatin in ⅓ c. of the strawberry juice. Dissolve over hot water. Add to buttermilk along with the remaining crushed berries, ½ c. sugar and lemon juice, stirring well to dissolve sugar.

Pour into two refrigerator trays or loaf pans. Freeze until mushy. Beat in mixing bowl until smooth. Return to refrigerator trays or pans. Freeze until firm. Garnish with whole berries. Makes 6 to 8 servings.

# DIFFERENT AND DELICIOUS

Avocado Sherbet plays a star role in a dinner meal. Start the meal with a few bites of this rich, mellow sherbet served in a hollowed out lime half.

Sour Cream Sherbet is a rosy beauty with a wonderful grape flavor. Perfect to serve by itself, or over pineapple chunks for a pink and gold dessert.

## AVOCADO SHERBET

*Be sure avocados are very ripe for this buttery, refreshing sherbet*

| | |
|---|---|
| 1 envelope unflavored gelatin | ⅛ tsp. salt |
| 2 tblsp. cold water | ¼ c. chopped pecans |
| ½ c. sugar | ½ c. orange juice |
| ½ c. milk | ¼ c. lemon juice |
| ⅔ c. mashed avocado | 1 egg white, stiffly beaten |

Soften gelatin in water; dissolve over boiling water. Dissolve sugar in milk. Add avocado, salt, pecans and juices. Stir in the gelatin.

Fold in beaten egg white. Freeze in refrigerator tray, stirring occasionally. Makes 4 to 6 servings.

## SOUR CREAM SHERBET

*Serve accompanied with fresh strawberries, cherries or raspberries*

| | |
|---|---|
| 1 c. dairy sour cream | 1 egg, well beaten |
| 1 c. milk | 1 c. grape juice |
| 1½ c. sugar | ¼ c. lemon juice |

Combine sour cream, milk, sugar, egg, grape juice and lemon juice in a large bowl; beat until sugar is dissolved. Pour into 2 refrigerator trays and freeze until nearly firm.

Turn mixture into chilled bowl. Beat until smooth and fluffy, but not melted, using chilled beater. Return to refrigerator trays and freeze until firm. Makes 6 servings.

# FRUIT FROSTS AND ICES

A magnificent Two-Tone Dessert, cool and pretty enough for company. A ripe red Cherry Ice that youngsters will love and Fruit Ice on Melon Circle that can be an elegant company treat— looks handsome but is simple to fix.

## TWO-TONE DESSERT

*Raspberries and lemons team up for this refreshing spring treat*

### RASPBERRY FROST

| | |
|---|---|
| 1 pt. raspberries | 1 envelope unflavored gelatin |
| ¾ c. unsweetened applesauce | ¼ c. cold water |
| 1 c. sugar | ¾ c. boiling water |

Put raspberries through food mill or electric blender to make purée. Add applesauce and sugar.

Soften gelatin in cold water, then dissolve in boiling water. Add to fruit mixture and blend. Pour into refrigerator tray and partially freeze.

Spoon partially frozen sherbet into large chilled bowl; beat until light and fluffy. Return to tray and freeze until firm.

### LEMON SHERBET

1 (14½ oz.) can evaporated milk, chilled
1 (6 oz.) can frozen lemonade concentrate
⅓ c. sugar

Place evaporated milk in chilled bowl; beat with chilled beater to consistency of whipped cream. Blend in lemonade concentrate and sugar. Pour into refrigerator tray and freeze.

To make dessert, half fill sherbet glasses with firm Raspberry Frost; fill remaining half with Lemon Sherbet. If you like, garnish with fresh raspberries and mint leaves. Makes 8 to 10 servings.

## Variations

**Green Gage Plum Frost:** Follow directions for Raspberry Frost, but use 2 c. purée made from cooked green gage plums instead of the raspberry and applesauce mixture. To serve, remove pits and cut into segments 6 fresh green gage plums. Place plums in dessert dishes and fill with frost. Makes 6 servings.

**Apple Frost in Pineapple Halves:** Follow directions for Raspberry Frost, omitting raspberries and increasing unsweetened applesauce to 2 c. Add a few drops green food color. To serve, cut 3 small pineapples in lengthwise halves. Hollow centers and fill with frost. Makes 6 servings.

**Three Fruit Sherbet:** Follow directions for Lemon Sherbet, but use only ⅔ can frozen lemonade concentrate; add 1 ripe banana, mashed, 15 maraschino cherries, finely chopped, and ⅓ c. sugar. Beat and freeze.

**Frost for Punch Bowl:** Follow recipe for Raspberry Frost to point where mixture is partially frozen and beaten. Then spoon into 8″ round layer cake pan and freeze until firm. Garnish with honeydew melon and cantaloupe balls and return to freezer until serving time. Unmold and decorate with fresh raspberries and mint leaves. Float on punch.

## CHERRY ICE

*Intriguing frosty red dessert—refreshing ending for a heavy meal*

| | |
|---|---|
| 2 c. frozen Ripe Red Cherry Purée (recipe follows) | 2 tblsp. water |
| | 2 tblsp. lemon juice |
| ¼ c. sugar | 1 egg white |
| 1 envelope unflavored gelatin | 2 tblsp. sugar |

Thaw Cherry Purée just enough to remove from freezer container. Add ¼ c. sugar to purée in saucepan; heat to just below boiling point.

Soften gelatin in water and lemon juice. Add to hot purée and stir until gelatin is dissolved. Cool. Pour into refrigerator trays and freeze until mushy (about 45 minutes). Remove from freezer, turn into bowl and beat well. Beat egg white until frothy; add sugar and beat until stiff peaks form. Fold into cherry mixture.

Return to refrigerator tray. Freeze 3 hours, stirring every 30 minutes. Makes 1 quart.

## RIPE RED CHERRY PURÉE

*Chill cherries at once after picking to keep their red color bright*

10 c. ripe, red cherries
¾ to 1 c. sugar for each 4 c. purée

Wash cherries and drain well. (You don't need to pit the cherries.) Place in heavy saucepan; cover. Heat 5 to 10 minutes until cherries are steaming and soft. Do not cook.

Place cherries in a colander, a small quantity at a time, and purée (cherry pits remain in the colander). Skim off the foam. Add sugar and stir to dissolve. (Riper cherries require the smaller amount of sugar.) Allow to cool to room temperature.

Freeze purée in 1 and 2 c. portions. Makes 4 cups.

## FRUIT ICE ON MELON CIRCLE

*Surprise your guests with this attractive way of serving melon*

| | |
|---|---|
| 1 peach | 1 c. water |
| 1 pear | Honeydew melon |
| ¼ c. lemon juice | Tokay (red) |
| ⅓ c. orange juice |    grape clusters |
| ⅔ c. sugar | |

Purée peach and pear by putting through food mill or electric blender. Add lemon juice, orange juice, sugar and water, beat until smooth.

Pour into refrigerator tray and freeze. To serve, cut fruit ice in cubes. Pile in center of honeydew melon circles (rind removed). Garnish with grape clusters. Makes 6 servings.

# CHAPTER 4

# Ice Cream Spectaculars

For extra-special occasions ice cream can take on an elegant air. Farm homemakers have been delighting their guests for years with their ice cream creations. There are ice cream layers alternated with cake, but you can go even more spectacular: How about a Meringue Ice Cream Mountain as a grande finale to a company meal? Strawberry Snowballs are a favorite birthday treat for one farm family and our Pink Party Pie always brings compliments.

For a wedding or shower, fix our Ice Cream Petit Fours—they are simply beautiful to look at and, best of all, can be made ahead of time. Cherry/Coconut Ice Cream Pie is a natural to serve on Valentine's Day or to top off Christmas Dinner. There are several beauties that are perfect for Christmas celebrations—the Candy Cane Ice Cream Loaf, for instance, or our scrumptious Mint-Frosted Cake Loaf.

You'll want to make the Cookie Shortcake—it's impressive as well as good eating.

Almost all these desserts can be made ahead of time and frozen until you are ready to serve. Spend a day preparing several of these luscious party treats and then you'll be proud to present your frozen masterpiece when company drops in on the spur of the moment.

## FROZEN ICE CREAM PIES

You can produce a show-stopper dessert with very little effort . . . all it takes is a pie shell—either the pastry or cookie-crumb variety— plus an ice cream filling and you have a beautiful dessert. Our Orange Ice Cream Pie and Cherry/Coconut Pie are perfect examples of finales that are easy from start to finish.

Now if you want a Grand Champion (which does take more

time but is worth every second) do try our Pink Party Pie . . . it's our version of Baked Alaska, cloud pink and glorious right down to the last crumb.

### ORANGE ICE CREAM PIE

*Second time around, try chocolate cookie crumbs for a new flavor*

| | |
|---|---|
| 2 c. gingersnap crumbs | 2 egg yolks, beaten |
| ½ c. melted butter | ¾ c. frozen orange juice |
| 2 c. sugar | concentrate, partially thawed |
| 1 c. water | 1 c. heavy cream |
| 1 c. light cream | |

Mix together crumbs and butter; press into 2 refrigerator trays and chill.

Combine sugar and water; bring to a boil and cook 8 minutes. Cool.

Scald light cream in double boiler; slowly add egg yolks. Cook over hot water, stirring constantly, until mixture is like soft custard. Remove from heat and cool.

Blend orange juice concentrate into cooled custard; combine with sugar syrup. Pour into 2 refrigerator trays (not the ones lined with crumbs). Freeze until firm.

Turn ice cream into chilled bowl; break into chunks. Beat until smooth.

Whip cream. Fold into ice cream. Pour into gingersnap crusts. Freeze until firm. Makes 10 servings.

N O T E : You can substitute 2 c. orange juice and 1½ tblsp. grated orange peel for the frozen concentrate.

### PINK PARTY PIE

*We rate this five gold stars . . . a luscious as well as lovely dessert*

| | |
|---|---|
| Baked 9″ Pink Pie Shell | 2 egg whites |
| (recipe follows) | ¼ tsp. cream of tartar |
| 1 qt. strawberry ice cream | ¼ c. sugar |
| 1 (10 oz.) pkg. frozen | Few drops red food color |
| strawberries | |

Pile softened ice cream into cool pie shell and spread evenly. Freeze overnight.

To serve, heat oven to extremely hot (500°).

Arrange berries over ice cream. Make meringue with egg whites, cream of tartar and sugar. Tint a delicate pink. Spread meringue over pie, covering filling completely so heat will not melt ice cream.

Set pie on wooden breadboard and bake about 5 minutes, or until lightly browned. Serve immediately.

## Variations

**Fresh Strawberry Pink Pie:** Substitute fresh for frozen berries. Place 2 c. ripe berries in baked pie shell, cover with 1 pt. vanilla ice cream and then with pink meringue. Brown meringue as directed for Pink Party Pie. Or use 1 c. each frozen strawberries and sliced peaches for an exotic pie.

## PINK PASTRY

*Good standard pastry recipe—you can of course omit the food color*

| | |
|---|---|
| 1 c. sifted flour | 3 to 4 drops red food color |
| ½ tsp. salt | 2 tblsp. water |
| ⅓ c. lard | |

Mix flour and salt; cut in lard with pastry blender. Add food color to water. Sprinkle on flour mixture and mix with a fork until all the flour is moistened. Gather the dough together and press firmly into a ball. Line pie pan with pastry; flute edges and prick pastry. Bake in hot oven (425°) 8 to 10 minutes. Cool. Makes enough pastry for 1 (8″ or 9″) one-crust pie.

N O T E : You can substitute ⅓ c. plus 1 tblsp. hydrogenated fat for the lard.

## CHERRY/COCONUT ICE CREAM PIE

*A new cherry pie from our Test Kitchens—perfect blend of flavors*

| | |
|---|---|
| 1⅓ c. flaked coconut | 1 qt. vanilla ice cream |
| 2 tblsp. melted butter | 1 c. Frozen Cherry Mix |
| ¼ c. graham cracker crumbs | (recipe follows) |
| 2 tblsp. sugar | |

Combine coconut and butter; mix well. Add crumbs and sugar, mixing thoroughly. Press firmly on bottom and sides of 8" pie pan. Bake in moderate oven (375°) 10 to 12 minutes, or until lightly browned. Cool.

Soften ice cream and spread in coconut shell. Spread slightly thawed Frozen Cherry Mix over top and freeze until ready to serve.

Thaw just enough to soften so that pie may be cut in wedges.

## FROZEN CHERRY MIX

*Use slightly thawed as topping for ice cream and cake*

| | |
|---|---|
| 5 qts. stemmed tart red cherries | 2 tsp. ground cinnamon |
| 2 (1 lb. 4 oz.) cans crushed pineapple, drained | ⅛ tsp. ground cloves |
| 8 c. sugar | 2 (1¾ oz.) pkgs. powdered fruit pectin |
| 8 tsp. ascorbic acid powder | |

Pit cherries, chop coarsely. (Fruit and juice should measure about 12 cups.)

Drain juice from cherries and reserve.

Add pineapple to cherries.

Combine sugar, ascorbic acid powder and spices. Add to cherries and pineapple; mix well. Let stand to dissolve sugar.

Combine pectin and cherry juice in large saucepan. Heat to a full rolling boil; boil 1 minute, stirring constantly. Add to cherry mixture; stir for 2 minutes. Ladle into containers. Seal. Allow to stand at room temperature until set (about 8 to 10 hours). Freeze. Makes 10 pints.

# FRENCH FRIED ICE CREAM—A NEW WONDER

Wait until you bring this super de luxe dessert to the table and then announce that the delicately browned ball that's warm on the outside and chillingly cold inside is French Fried Ice Cream! And you can fix this conversation piece dessert ahead of time and freeze in individually foil-wrapped balls. It only takes 30 seconds to cook after it's dropped in the deep hot fat.

Serve immediately in its own golden crumbed jacket or top with sweetened fresh strawberries or a generous pour of hot fudge sauce. Your dessert will be the talk of the neighborhood.

## FRENCH FRIED ICE CREAM

*A wonderful surprise to serve at a party topped with fudge sauce*

2 eggs, beaten
2 tblsp. milk
1 qt. vanilla ice cream

1 c. pound cake crumbs
Salad oil

Combine eggs and milk.

Take a scoop of ice cream, and roll it in crumbs. Pack crumbs firmly with hands. Dip in egg-milk mixture, then roll again in crumbs and pack firmly. Wrap in plastic wrap or aluminum foil and freeze. Repeat procedure, making 6 ice cream balls.

Heat oil to 320° in 2-qt. saucepan (use enough oil to fill pan one third full). Place ice cream ball in hot oil and keep turning quickly with large fork until uniformly brown, about 30 seconds. Serve immediately. Makes 6 servings.

## MERINGUE ICE CREAM MOUNTAIN

*Meringues with a new twist . . . baked in two layers and served with vanilla ice cream topped with juicy strawberries in between*

3 egg whites
½ tsp. cream of tartar
1 c. sugar
1 tsp. vinegar
½ tsp. vanilla

1 qt. vanilla ice cream
2 c. sweetened fresh strawberries
or 2 (10 oz.) pkgs. frozen
strawberries, thawed

Combine egg whites and cream of tartar. Beat until soft peaks form. Add sugar, 1 tblsp. at a time, beating well after each addition to dissolve sugar. Add vinegar and vanilla and continue beating to the stiff-peak stage.

Line two baking sheets with heavy brown paper. Draw 12 (3") circles on one, 12 (1½") circles on the other. Spread meringue thinly in each circle. Make peaks on 12 smaller circles from remaining meringue.

Bake in slow oven (300°) 20 minutes; reduce heat to very

slow (250°) and bake 15 minutes longer. Turn off heat; leave meringue in oven to dry.

Lift gently from paper with spatula. Place large meringues on serving platter. Spoon on ice cream. Top with strawberries. Place small meringues on top. Makes 12 servings.

## ICE CREAM PETITS FOURS

*Surprise—they're ice cream not cake and so easy to prepare ahead*

*To Use Brick Ice Cream:*

On chilled metal tray, set over pan of ice, cut half-gallon bricks of ice cream into 24 squares, or 18 diamonds, or 16 rectangles. Place on individual pieces of waxed paper. Freeze firm at least 24 hours.

Whip 2 c. heavy cream; divide in fourths. Tint one a delicate pink, one green, one yellow; leave one white.

Work on chilled tray over ice. Remove ice cream from freezer one piece at a time; frost with whipped cream; decorate with tiny candies or pastel-colored decorating sugars, nuts or whipped cream designs. (You can leave some petits fours unfrosted and roll sides in tinted coconut or finely chopped nuts.) Return to freezer immediately so they will hold shape.

When petits fours are frozen firm, transfer to cupcake papers; package in flat box. Wrap, and freeze.

*To Use Bulk or Homemade Ice Cream:*

Place 6″ strip of heavy-duty aluminum foil in bottom of 8″ square pan with ends of foil extending over edges of pan. Pack ½ gallon soft ice cream evenly in pan; freeze until very firm. Turn ice cream out of pan onto chilled tray set over pan of ice. Proceed as directed for brick ice cream.

To make round shapes, pack ice cream in 6-oz. juice cans; freeze firm. Cut other end out of can; push out ice cream and cut in half. Decorate according to directions for brick ice cream.

## ICE CREAM SURPRISES

*Luscious and lovely ice cream desserts for very special occasions*

**Ice Cream in Orange Shells:** Pack ice cream or sherbet into scooped-out orange shells, then freeze. Do this a day or two ahead. Green leaf garnish gives a fresh-from-the-grove look.

**Buffet Party Dessert:** The day before your party, scoop ice cream balls onto a cold metal tray; return to freezer to firm up. Chill your prettiest *metal* bowl; fill it with ice cream balls; put bowl in freezer. At serving time, add nuts and fruits. Guests make their own sundaes. No last-minute scooping.

**Ice Cream Birthday Cake:** Pack ice cream into a 9″ springform cake pan, return to freezer. Next day decorate like a cake, with candles. For a fancier cake, line the pan with vanilla ice cream, and freeze it hard. Then freeze scoops of different flavors, and use them—along with more vanilla—to fill in center of lined pan. Sprinkle colored sugar over a paper cut-out design on top, and add candy to decorate base of cake.

## MINT SHERBET RING

*Heap center of this pale green mold with plump, glossy blackberries*

| | |
|---|---|
| 6 sprigs mint | ½ c. milk |
| ¾ c. sugar | ½ c. lemon juice |
| Dash of salt | 2 egg whites |
| 1 c. water | ¼ c. sugar |

Crush mint; combine with ¾ c. sugar, salt and water in saucepan. Simmer 5 minutes; cool and strain. Add milk and lemon juice. Pour into refrigerator tray and freeze until firm.

Beat egg whites until foamy. Gradually add ¼ c. sugar and continue beating until mixture stands in peaks.

Turn frozen mixture into bowl and break into chunks. Beat until smooth. Fold in egg whites. Put quickly into a chilled 1-qt. ring mold; freeze until firm. Makes 6 servings.

## *ANGEL FOOD DELIGHTS*

Angel food cake and ice cream combine to make a dramatic dessert team. Here are four ways to create masterpieces that you will be proud to serve at your finest dinner party. All are make-aheads.

## FROZEN MINT-FROSTED CAKE LOAF

*You can skip the freezing and serve dessert as soon as it's made, but it's nice to have on hand*

1 (15 or 16 oz.) pkg. angel
    food cake mix
1 qt. brick strawberry ice cream
1 c. heavy cream, whipped

3 tblsp. confectioners sugar
¼ tsp. peppermint extract
4 to 6 drops green food color

Bake cake according to package directions in two 9×5×3" loaf pans. Cool.

Split 1 loaf into 3 lengthwise slices (freeze other loaf for use later).

Cut ice cream into 7 equal slices.

Cover bottom cake layer with 3½ slices ice cream; top with middle cake layer; cover with remaining ice cream; top with third cake layer.

Blend whipped cream, sugar, extract and food color; use to frost sides and top of cake.

Let cake set a few minutes after you frost it; freeze uncovered until firm. Remove from freezer; wrap and return to freezer. Cake will keep about 8 weeks. Makes 8 servings.

NOTE: You can substitute chocolate ice cream for the strawberry.

## STRAWBERRY ANGEL CAKE

*Strawberries, ice cream and angel cake make this pretty dessert*

1 (8") round angel food cake
2½ c. boiling water
2 (3 oz.) pkgs. strawberry
    flavor gelatin
1 (10 oz.) pkg. frozen sliced
    strawberries

⅛ tsp. salt
2 tsp. lemon juice
1 pt. vanilla ice cream
2 c. fresh strawberries
1 c. heavy cream or 1 envelope
    dessert topping mix

Mold this dessert in the bowl in which you mix your ingredients. To find right size, turn cake upside down in bowl—it should fit loosely. (Try a 3-qt. size.)

Measure boiling water into bowl; add gelatin. Stir to dissolve.

Add frozen berries, salt and lemon juice. Break apart with fork or spoon as berries thaw.

Add ice cream; break apart. Stir, blending into mixture as it melts.

In a matter of minutes the gelatin mixture will start to thicken. Push cake upside down, into middle of mixture. Lay a piece of waxed paper over top. Place small plate over cake; then put a light weight on plate (use just enough weight to keep the cake immersed; overweighting will make it too compact). Chill. Remove weight when gelatin sets (about 15 minutes).

To unmold, set bowl in hot water 2 or 3 minutes. Run spatula around side; invert on serving plate.

Whip cream. Garnish entire mold with whipped cream and fresh berries. Or cut into wedges and serve wedges on individual plates with whipped cream and fresh berries. Makes 10 to 12 servings.

## ICE CREAM LAYER CAKE

*Use your family's favorite flavor of ice cream for this treat*

| | |
|---|---|
| 1 (10″) angel food, sponge or chiffon cake | 1 tblsp. sugar |
| | 1 tsp. vanilla |
| 1 qt. ice cream | 1 (3½ oz.) can flaked or shredded coconut |
| 2 c. heavy cream | |

Cut cake lengthwise into 3 layers. Spread ice cream between layers. Place cake in freezer to harden.

Whip cream; add sugar and vanilla; use to frost top and sides of cake. Cover with coconut; return to freezer until whipped cream is hard. Wrap in freezer paper; freeze.

To serve, slice without thawing. Serve at once. Makes 16 to 20 servings.

## ICE CREAM CAKE

*A dazzling party cake—colorful as confetti and delicious, too*

| | |
|---|---|
| 1 (10″) angel food cake | 1 qt. pistachio ice cream |
| 1 qt. strawberry ice cream | 2 c. heavy cream |
| 1 qt. chocolate ice cream | |

Cut cool cake, made from packaged mix or bakery bought, cross-wise in 4 equal layers.

Spread tops of 3 bottom layers with ice cream, using a different flavor for each. (You can choose your favorites.) Do one at a time, starting with strawberry, and place immediately in freezer. Proceed with chocolate ice cream; stack on top of strawberry in freezer. Then follow with layer spread with pistachio ice cream. Add top layer of cake. Work fast.

Whip cream and use to frost cake. Store in freezer until serving time. (May be made several days ahead.) Makes 20 servings.

# ICE CREAM DESSERTS

Take softened ice cream and combine it with some interesting ingredients and you have a company dessert. In Vanilla Almond Crunch, the ice cream is spread over a chewy base and decorated with almonds. The ice cream is stirred into the recipe for Velvety Lime Squares, producing a tart, tangy, textured dessert. Strawberry Snowballs are a cinch to make; all you do is roll balls of ice cream in coconut, freeze. Serve on a crimson bed of partly thawed frozen strawberries.

## VANILLA ALMOND CRUNCH

*Try a splash of chocolate sauce on it for a special sundae*

1 (4 oz.) pkg. slivered almonds
¼ c. melted butter
1 c. crushed rice cereal squares
½ c. light brown sugar, firmly packed
½ c. flaked coconut
⅛ tsp. salt
2 qts. vanilla ice cream, softened

Toast almonds in melted butter. Remove half of almonds from butter and set aside.

Combine crushed cereal, brown sugar, coconut and salt with remaining almonds and butter. Pat mixture gently into 13×9×2″ pan. Bake in moderate (375°) oven 5 minutes. Cool.

Spread ice cream over cooled crust. Decorate top with reserved almonds. Freeze until firm. Cover tightly, and return to freezer. Makes 10 servings.

## VELVETY LIME SQUARES

*Top each serving of this pastel green dessert with a pecan half*

1 (3 oz.) can flaked coconut
½ c. vanilla wafer crumbs
2 tblsp. melted butter
2 tblsp. sugar
2 (3 oz.) pkgs. lime flavor
    gelatin
2 c. boiling water

1 (6 oz.) can frozen limeade
    concentrate
Few drops green food color
1 qt. plus 1 pt. vanilla ice
    cream, softened
⅛ tsp. salt

Carefully toast ½ c. coconut in moderate (375°) oven until lightly browned, about 5 minutes. Set aside.

Combine remaining coconut, crumbs, butter and sugar. Lightly press into 11×7×1½" pan and bake in moderate oven (375°) 6 to 7 minutes. Cool.

Dissolve gelatin in boiling water. Add limeade concentrate, food color, ice cream and salt; stir until dissolved. Pour into crust. Top with reserved toasted coconut and garnish with pecans, if you wish. Freeze until firm. Cover tightly. Return to freezer.

Remove dessert from freezer 20 minutes before cutting. Makes 6 to 8 servings.

## STRAWBERRY SNOWBALLS

*These are easy to make but look lovely on a Christmas party table*

½ gal. vanilla ice cream
1½ c. flaked coconut
2 (1 lb.) pkgs. frozen whole strawberries

Using small scoop, make balls of ice cream. Set each ball as shaped on tray in freezer.

Spread coconut on large sheet of waxed paper. Roll ice cream balls in coconut to coat lightly. Return to freezer. When firm, package and keep in freezer.

To serve, partly thaw strawberries in a large shallow serving dish. Top with snowballs; garnish each with a berry. Makes 10 to 12 servings.

NOTE: For a change, arrange snowballs on raspberry sherbet and spoon on a little partly thawed frozen orange juice concentrate. Or serve snowballs with your favorite chocolate sauce (may be made from instant chocolate frosting mix following package directions).

# BEAUTIFUL BOMBES

When you want to serve an extraordinary and elegant dessert, make any of these five bombes. A bombe sounds fancy but it's merely a combination of ice cream flavors (two or more) and sometimes crumbs that are layered in a mold, with the outside layer being a different flavor of ice cream than the inner. They are time-consuming but not difficult to prepare. Choose your prettiest mold and set to work to create a de luxe dessert. The secret is to work quickly so that the ice cream will not melt. Once you have tried these, then go on to invent your own ice cream flavor combinations.

### STRAWBERRY/ORANGE BOMBE

*This delightful frozen party dessert features a tangy orange-flavored center covered with a pink strawberry ice cream layer*

| | |
|---|---|
| 1 qt. strawberry ice cream, slightly softened | 2 tblsp. orange juice |
| 2 egg yolks | 1 tblsp. cold water |
| ⅓ c. sugar | 1 egg white |
| 1 tblsp. grated orange peel | 2 tblsp. sugar |
| | 1 c. heavy cream, whipped |

Chill a 7-c. mold in freezer. Quickly spread softened ice cream as evenly as possible with back of spoon or spatula on inside of mold to make a shell lining about ½″ thick. Return to freezer to harden.

Meanwhile, in top of double boiler beat egg yolks well. Beat in ⅓ c. sugar, orange peel and juice and water. Cook over rapidly boiling water, stirring constantly, until thickened (about 10 minutes). Cool completely.

In a small mixing bowl beat egg white until frothy. Gradually beat in 2 tblsp. sugar; beat until stiff peaks form. Fold in orange mixture; then whipped cream. Pour into ice cream-lined mold. Freeze.

To unmold, dip into lukewarm water and turn out onto chilled plate. Return to freezer to harden. To serve, garnish with fresh or frozen strawberries. Makes 8 to 10 servings.

## CINNAMON/COFFEE BOMBE

*Cinnamon and coffee join with chocolate for a company dessert*

2 c. vanilla wafer crumbs
½ c. flaked coconut
¼ c. melted butter
½ tsp. ground cinnamon
1 qt. coffee ice cream, slightly
    softened

⅓ c. chopped salted nuts
1 pt. chocolate ice cream,
    slightly softened

Combine vanilla wafer crumbs, coconut, butter and cinnamon. Press evenly and firmly against bottom and sides of 7-c. mold. Freeze.

Quickly spread coffee ice cream as evenly as possible with back of spoon or spatula over crumb mixture. Press salted nuts into ice cream. Return to freezer to harden. Spoon chocolate ice cream into center to fill mold. Freeze.

To unmold, dip into lukewarm water and turn mold out onto chilled plate. Return to freezer to harden. Makes 10 to 12 servings.

## CHOCOLATE MINT BOMBE

*A three-layer ice cream treat circled by chocolate wafer crumbs*

1½ c. chocolate wafer crumbs
¼ c. melted butter
1 pt. vanilla ice cream, slightly
    softened
1 pt. chocolate chip mint ice
    cream, slightly softened

1 pt. butter pecan ice cream,
    softened
4 to 5 whole cherries
    (quartered)

Combine crumbs and butter; press evenly and firmly against bottom and sides of 6-c. mold. Freeze.

Spread vanilla ice cream evenly with back of spoon over crumb shell. Freeze. Repeat with chocolate chip mint ice cream. Freeze. Spoon in ½ pt. butter pecan. Press maraschino cherries into ice cream. Spoon remaining ice cream in center. Freeze.

Unmold by dipping into warm water and turn out onto chilled plate. Return to freezer to harden. Makes 10 to 12 servings.

## PISTACHIO CRUNCH BOMBE

*Guests will marvel at this beautiful frozen dessert*

| | |
|---|---|
| ¾ c. corn flake crumbs | 1 qt. vanilla ice cream, |
| ½ c. flaked coconut | slightly softened |
| ¼ c. chopped toasted peanuts | 1 pt. pistachio ice cream, |
| ¼ c. sugar | slightly softened |
| ¼ c. butter, softened | |

Combine corn flake crumbs, coconut, peanuts, sugar and butter. Press onto bottom and sides of 7-c. mold.

Spread vanilla ice cream as evenly as possible with back of spoon or spatula on inside of crumb shell. Place in freezer to harden ice cream. Spoon pistachio ice cream into center to fill mold. Freeze.

Unmold by dipping into warm water and turn out onto chilled plate. Place back in freezer to harden. Serve with your favorite chocolate sauce. Makes 10 to 12 servings.

## GINGER/ORANGE BOMBE

*A lovely make-ahead frozen dessert that will always win praise*

| | |
|---|---|
| 2⅔ c. gingersnap crumbs | ⅓ c. coarsely chopped walnuts |
| 2 tblsp. sugar | 1 pt. orange sherbet |
| ¼ c. butter, slightly softened | |
| 1 qt. vanilla ice cream, | |
| softened | |

Combine gingersnap crumbs, sugar and butter. Press onto bottom and sides of a 6-c. mold.

Spread vanilla ice cream as evenly as possible with back of spoon or spatula about 1″ thick over crumb shell. Press walnuts into bottom and sides of ice cream. Place in freezer to harden ice cream.

Spoon orange sherbet into center to fill mold. Freeze.

Unmold by dipping into warm water and turn out onto chilled plate. Place back in freezer to harden. Makes 10 to 12 servings.

# POTPOURRI OF ICE CREAM DESSERTS

Farm women are noted for using their imagination and these recipes do just that. There's a dessert for every occasion. All are quick and easy, yet are a new idea for serving ice cream.

## COOKIE SHORTCAKE

*Red and white candy makes the dessert colorful—it also tastes good*

24 chocolate wafer cookies (about ½ lb.)
1 qt. vanilla ice cream
½ c. crushed peppermint stick candy

Place a cookie on each dessert plate. Top with spoonful ice cream and sprinkle with 1 tsp. candy; top with another cookie. Press down gently on top cookie, add a second spoonful of ice cream, sprinkle with more candy, and cover with a third cookie.

Serve at once with ice cream, candy sprinkled on top; or store in freezer until serving time. Makes 8 servings.

## CANDY CANE ICE CREAM LOAF

*For added decoration, arrange candy canes across top of loaf*

3 eggs
1¼ c. sugar
6 c. milk
1 pt. light cream
1 (15 oz.) can sweetened
  condensed milk (not
  evaporated)

2 tblsp. vanilla
1 c. crushed hard peppermint
  candy

Beat eggs until light. Gradually add sugar, beating until thick. Add remaining ingredients, except candy. Pour into 1-gal. freezer can. Freeze by basic directions (see "Freezing and Ripening Ice Cream" in Index).

Add candy after freezing. Working quickly to avoid melting, pack ice cream in three 9×5×3" foil-lined loaf pans. Freeze until firm. Makes 1 gallon.

## ECLAIRS

*Fill with coffee ice cream and served with chocolate sauce*

| | |
|---|---|
| 1 c. milk | ¼ tsp. salt |
| ½ c. butter | 4 eggs |
| 1 c. sifted flour | Vanilla ice cream |

Heat milk; add butter. Bring to boil. Add flour and salt all at once. Cook until batter leaves sides of pan and forms a ball. Remove from heat; cool.

Add eggs, one at a time, beating thoroughly after each.

Place spoonfuls of batter in 3″ ovals about 2″ apart on greased baking sheet, heaping them well in center. Bake in hot oven (400°) about 10 to 15 minutes until points are light brown; reduce heat to slow (325°) about 15 minutes, until puffs are done.

Cool puffs; cut slit in the side of each. Fill with ice cream and freeze. Serve in cupcake papers with a choice of sauces. Makes 18 eclairs.


## JELLY ROLL PARFAIT

*Try to keep these ingredients on hand for a last-minute dessert*

| | |
|---|---|
| ½ c. sugar | 1 c. hot water |
| 1½ c. sliced fresh strawberries | 1 pt. vanilla ice cream |
| 1 pkg. strawberry flavor gelatin | 1 jelly roll cake |

Add sugar to berries. Let stand.

Dissolve gelatin in hot water. Gradually add spoonfuls of ice cream, stirring until melted. Add strawberries and juice. Let stand while preparing mold.

Cut jelly roll into eight ½″ slices. Place 6 slices around sides of 8½ × 4½ × 2½″ loaf pan.

Pour strawberry mixture into pan carefully. Place remaining jelly roll slices over top. Chill until firm, about 3 hours.

To remove, run spatula around edge and turn out on serving plate. Makes 8 to 10 servings.

NOTE: You can use 1 (10 oz.) pkg. frozen strawberries, thawed, for the fresh berries, but omit the sugar and decrease amount of water to ¾ c.

## PARTY PARFAIT

*A mouth-watering way to serve watermelon and ice cream*

2 qts. Mint Ice Cream 8 mint sprigs
4 c. watermelon cubes
24 watermelon sticks, cut from
  rind into center of melon

Pack one third of ice cream into 8 chilled parfait glasses; top with melon cubes. Spoon on additional ice cream.
Insert melon sticks and garnish with mint sprigs. Makes 8 servings.

## PEACH SUNDAE

*You can get this tempting dessert ready in the twinkling of an eye*

1 (1 lb. 13 oz.) can cling peaches
1 pt. vanilla ice cream
1 c. maple blended syrup

Place peach halves, cut side up, into individual dessert dishes. Top each with a spoonful of ice cream. Pour syrup over all. Serve immediately. Makes 6 to 8 servings.

## FRUIT AND SHERBET COCKTAIL

*An attractive appetizer that is simple to prepare at the last minute*

1 (1 lb. 14 oz.) can pineapple chunks, chilled
1 (10 or 11 oz.) can mandarin oranges, chilled
1 pt. lime sherbet

Drain fruits. Half fill glasses with pineapple chunks; top with scoop of sherbet. Fill around sherbet with orange sections. Makes 6 servings.

## MAYPOLE ICE CREAM

*A delightful way to serve ice cream for a children's birthday party*

Spoon 2 half-gallons vanilla ice cream into 25 (5 oz.) yellow paper dessert dishes. Place on baking sheets or shallow pans. Set in freezer immediately. When ice cream is frozen, cover tightly.

Make "ribbon poles" by inserting thin ribbons of various colors into colored soda straws. Fasten with a little glue. Fold protruding ends of ribbons back against straw. At serving time, drop candy sprinkles over ice cream. Stick a "pole" in center of each serving. Makes 25 servings.

## CHOCOLATE DESSERT CUPS

*Make ahead; add scoops of ice cream or sherbet at serving time*

Melt 2 tblsp. semisweet chocolate pieces at a time over hot (not boiling) water. As soon as melted, spread chocolate over inside of fluted cupcake papers. Set in muffin-pan cups; freeze at once until firm, about 15 minutes; peel off paper and return cups to freezer until ready to serve.

At serving time, fill cups with ice cream or sherbet and garnish with fruit. One (6 oz.) pkg. semisweet chocolate pieces makes about 8 cups.

# CHAPTER 5

# Sauces Make It Special

Even though we think every ice cream and cake recipe is special by itself, sometimes it is fun to experiment and add a bit of glamour by dressing up your cake or ice cream.

We have a variety of sauces and toppings in this chapter that you will want to try. In fact, many can be made ahead and stored in your refrigerator. Then you are ready to produce a de luxe dessert in a few minutes.

For those who demand super sundaes, after they have helped themselves to the sauce of their choice, pass a bowl of whipped cream and a bowl of chopped nuts.

## FRUIT SAUCES

Homemade ice cream is delicious just plain Jane, but it can really be made extra-special by adding a homemade sauce. These fruit sauces dress up basic vanilla ice cream. Make several of the flavors and set up a sauce bar; let everyone ladle on his own.

### APRICOT SAUCE

*Try this sauce on a scoop of vanilla ice cream or warm gingerbread*

| | |
|---|---|
| 2 tblsp. cornstarch | ½ c. light corn syrup |
| Dash of ground nutmeg | 2 tsp. lemon juice |
| Dash of salt | ¼ tsp. grated lemon peel |
| 1 (12 oz.) can apricot nectar | |

Combine cornstarch, nutmeg and salt in small saucepan. Gradually blend in apricot nectar and corn syrup. Bring to a boil over medium heat and boil 1 minute, stirring constantly. Remove from heat; stir in lemon juice and peel. Serve warm over plain cake or ice cream. Makes 2 cups.

## APRICOT RUM SAUCE

*Layer ice cream and sauce in parfait glasses and top with pecans*

1 (1 lb. 1 oz.) can whole apricots

2½ tblsp. cornstarch

1 c. light corn syrup

¼ c. orange juice

Pinch of salt

½ tsp. rum extract

½ tsp. grated orange peel

Drain liquid from apricots, adding water, if necessary to make 1 cup. Press apricots through fine sieve.

Place cornstarch in medium saucepan. Gradually blend in apricot liquid and apricot purée. Stir in corn syrup, orange juice and salt. Bring to a boil over medium heat and boil 1 minute, stirring constantly. Remove from heat; stir in rum extract and orange peel. Serve warm over plain cake or ice cream. Makes 2½ cups.

## SPICY BLUEBERRY SAUCE

*Spoon over lemon sherbet for a cool snack on a warm evening*

1 (10 oz.) pkg. frozen blueberries, thawed

½ c. light corn syrup

1 tblsp. cornstarch

1 tblsp. water

⅛ tsp. ground cinnamon

⅛ tsp. ground allspice

Dash of salt

2 tblsp. lemon juice

Combine blueberries and corn syrup in medium saucepan.

Blend cornstarch and water; stir into blueberry mixture. Add cinnamon, allspice and salt. Bring to a boil over medium heat and boil 1 minute, stirring constantly. Remove from heat; stir in lemon juice. Serve warm over plain cake or ice cream. Makes 1½ cups.

## BLUEBERRY SAUCE

*Accompany with slices of lemon chiffon cake topped with ice cream*

1 tblsp. cornstarch

½ c. sugar

¼ tsp. salt

½ c. water

3 c. unsweetened blueberries

Mix cornstarch, sugar and salt in a small saucepan. Add water and stir until sugar is dissolved. Stir in blueberries.

Cook over medium heat, stirring constantly, until sauce is slightly thickened and clear. Makes about 2 cups.

## LEMON/BLUEBERRY SAUCE

*Topping for vanilla ice cream—good over angel food cake, too*

1 (10 oz.) pkg. frozen
   blueberries
½ c. pineapple juice
¼ c. water
¼ c. sugar

1 tblsp. cornstarch
⅛ tsp. salt
¼ tsp. grated lemon peel
1 tsp. lemon juice

Combine blueberries, pineapple juice, water, sugar, cornstarch, salt and lemon peel in 1-qt. saucepan. Cook, stirring, over medium heat until sauce thickens. Cool slightly; stir in lemon juice. Chill. Makes about 1¾ cups.

## CHERRY SAUCE

*This fruit sauce can be made ahead and reheated at serving time*

1 (1 lb.) can pitted sour red
   cherries
2 tblsp. cornstarch
⅛ tsp. cinnamon

Dash of salt
1 c. light corn syrup
12 drops red food coloring
½ tsp. almond flavoring

Drain and reserve liquid from cherries, adding water, if necessary, to make ⅔ c.

Combine cornstarch, cinnamon and salt in medium saucepan. Gradually blend in cherry liquid; add cherries. Stir in corn syrup. Bring to a boil over medium heat and boil 1 minute, stirring constantly. Add red food coloring and almond flavoring. Serve warm over ice cream or plain cake. Makes 2¾ cups.

## ORANGE CREAM SAUCE

*Keep this tangy, smooth sauce in your refrigerator for quick desserts*

6 egg yolks
⅔ c. sugar
⅔ c. orange juice
2 tsp. grated orange peel

1 tsp. grated lemon peel
⅛ tsp. salt
2 tblsp. lemon juice
½ pt. dairy sour cream (1 c.)

Lightly beat egg yolks in top of double boiler. Blend in the remaining ingredients except the sour cream. Cook, stirring constantly, over simmering (not boiling) water until thick, about 15 minutes. Chill.

Stir until smooth; blend in sour cream. Spoon on sliced cake. Garnish with orange slices. Makes about 3 cups.

NOTE: If you want to serve a thicker sauce, refrigerate it several hours after you add the sour cream.

## FRIENDSHIP TOPPING

Legend has it that this brandied fruit was started more than 200 years ago (1761) in France by the mother of Napoleon I of France. This is a rough translation of the directions that accompanied it: When this "starter" is given to you . . . it is given with love and it must be shared with others. We suggest that you keep it in an 8-cup apothecary jar with a lid which fits loosely in order to allow the air to circulate. This fruit must never be stored in a sealed jar and the contents must never fall below the 2-cup amount or the fermentation will stop and the fruit will spoil. Keep at room temperature in an open, light area. Add fruit to the starter after 2 weeks have passed but never before. Always use well drained, solid, canned fruit.

We decided to try originating some of this topping in our Countryside Test Kitchens so you wouldn't have to wait for a "starter" gift that might never come. And, of course, (Mother Bonaparte Napoleon to the contrary notwithstanding, it works!) Here's the recipe to "start" your own Friendship Topping. When you have 2 cups of the mixture to share, carry on the nice custom and give a "start" to a friend or neighbor.

## FRIENDSHIP STARTER

⅓ c. canned peaches, cut in chunks

⅓ c. canned apricots, cut in chunks

⅓ c. canned pineapple, cut in chunks

¼ c. maraschino cherries, cut in wedges

1 c. granulated sugar

Combine all ingredients in apothecary jar, stirring well. Stir about once a week. Every 14 days add 1 c. sugar and 1 c. canned fruit of your choice or add ⅓ c. each of 3 different kinds of fruit. Do not add juice; do not use fresh fruit; DO NOT REFRIGERATE. Keep a card near your Friendship Topping to record dates and type of fruit added. In fact, why not jot down "add to Friendship Topping" every two weeks on your calendar as a reminder.

This potent topping is a conversation piece over vanilla ice cream!

# ASSORTED SAUCES

Many times it's the sauce that makes the difference. We have some mouthwatering sauces to be poured over ice creams. Burnt-Sugar Sauce over chocolate ice cream is a heavenly treat. Easy Butterscotch Sauce eats well over vanilla or butter pecan. You'll love the Coffee/Pecan Sauce ladled over coffee ice cream for double strength flavor. Chocolate, Peanut/Chocolate and just plain Peanut Sauce are great over ice cream and cake. Mix and match your own flavor combinations.

## BURNT-SUGAR SUNDAE SAUCE

*Makes just plain vanilla ice cream a royal dessert fit for a king*

¼ c. hot water
½ c. Burnt-Sugar Syrup (recipe follows)

¼ c. chopped nuts
¼ c. candied ginger, minced, or orange or lemon peel

Combine all ingredients. Chill. Serve over vanilla ice cream. Makes enough for 6 sundaes.

## BURNT-SUGAR SYRUP

2 c. sugar
1 c. boiling water

Pour sugar in heavy skillet that heats uniformly. Melt over low heat, stirring constantly with wooden spoon to prevent scorching (don't worry about the lumps—they'll melt away).

When sugar becomes a clear, brown syrup, remove from heat.

Stir in boiling water, slowly so that it doesn't spatter. Return to low heat, and stir until syrup is smooth again. Cool.

Pour into clean pint jar, cover tightly, and store at room temperature. Keeps 6 to 8 weeks. Makes 1⅓ cups.

## EASY BUTTERSCOTCH SAUCE

*This golden rich sauce is delicious served either warm or cold*

1¼ c. light brown sugar, firmly
  packed
1 c. light corn syrup
¼ c. butter

¼ tsp. salt
½ c. evaporated milk
1 tsp. vanilla
½ c. toasted chopped walnuts

Mix together brown sugar, corn syrup, butter and salt in 1-qt. saucepan. Cook over medium heat, stirring constantly, until sugar dissolves. Do not boil. Cool to room temperature.

Stir in milk and vanilla, beating with spoon until well mixed. Add walnuts. Makes 2½ cups.

## BUTTERSCOTCH ICE CREAM SAUCE

*Dark brown sugar and corn syrup make this definitely butterscotch*

1 c. dark brown sugar, firmly
  packed
⅓ c. dark corn syrup
¼ c. water
¼ c. butter

⅓ c. light cream or evaporated
  milk
Dash of salt
½ tsp. vanilla

Combine brown sugar, corn syrup, water and butter in saucepan. Bring to a boil and cook, stirring occasionally, to the soft ball stage (236° on candy thermometer). This takes about 4 minutes. Remove from heat and let cool slightly.

Add light cream, salt and vanilla. Beat well. Serve warm or cold. Makes 1 cup.

## COFFEE/PECAN SAUCE

*Pour over coffee ice cream for a double-strength coffee flavor*

1 tblsp. instant coffee
2 tsp. cornstarch
½ c. water

½ c. dark corn syrup
1 tsp. grated orange peel
½ c. chopped pecans

Mix coffee and cornstarch in small saucepan; gradually stir in water. Add corn syrup and orange peel. Cook over medium heat, stirring constantly, until sauce comes to boil. Reduce heat and simmer 1 minute. Remove from heat. Stir in pecans. Cool. Cover and chill. Serve over ice cream and/or plain cake. Makes about 1 cup.

## CHOCOLATE ICE CREAM SAUCE

*Nothing like a chocolate sundae to delight children—keep this on hand*

| | |
|---|---|
| 2 squares unsweetened chocolate | ¼ tsp. salt |
| 1¼ c. light cream | 1 tblsp. butter |
| ¾ c. sugar | 1 tsp. vanilla |
| 3 tblsp. flour | |

Combine chocolate and light cream in top of double boiler. Cook over boiling water, stirring occasionally, until smooth.

Combine sugar, flour and salt. Add enough hot mixture to make a smooth paste. Combine paste with hot mixture in double boiler. Cook until smooth and slightly thick, about 10 minutes. Remove from heat; add butter and vanilla. Serve hot or cold. Makes 2 cups.

## PEANUT ICE CREAM SAUCE

*Store in covered container in refrigerator . . . stir before serving*

| | |
|---|---|
| 1 c. dark corn syrup | ½ c. milk |
| 1 c. sugar | ½ tsp. vanilla |
| ¼ tsp. salt | ½ c. chopped, roasted salted |
| 2 tblsp. butter or regular margarine | peanuts |

Combine corn syrup, sugar, salt, butter and milk in a saucepan. Place over medium heat, stirring constantly until mixture begins to boil. Boil gently 3 minutes, stirring occasionally. Stir in vanilla and peanuts. Cool. Makes 2 cups.

## PEANUT/CHOCOLATE SAUCE

*Keep chocolate pudding mix on hand for this jiffy ice cream sauce*

1 (4 oz.) pkg. chocolate pudding
and pie filling mix
¾ c. water
¾ c. light corn syrup
¼ tsp. salt

1 tblsp. butter or regular
margarine
⅓ c. peanut butter
½ tsp. vanilla

Empty package contents into saucepan. Gradually add water, mixing until smooth. Add corn syrup and salt; mix well.

Cook over medium heat, stirring constantly until mixture comes to a boil.

Remove from heat and add butter, peanut butter and vanilla; stir until melted. Serve warm or cold over ice cream. Makes 1¾ cups.

# VARIATION TOPPINGS

All of these toppings were developed for spooning over cakes, though we see no reason why you might not like to try a spoonful over ice cream. Busy day ahead? Then mix together the Fast-Fix Fruit Topping or the Orange Syrup and drizzle over cake or cubes of cake that have been layered in a parfait glass.

## FAST-FIX FRUIT TOPPING

*Topping keeps well in refrigerator—handy to dress up cake slices*

1 (1 lb. 4½ oz.) can pineapple chunks
1 (11 oz.) can mandarin oranges
1 c. orange marmalade

Drain fruits; stir in marmalade. Heat and serve warm or cold on angel cake slices. Makes 3 cups.

## ORANGE SYRUP

*Can be stored in refrigerator for several weeks—always handy*

1 (6 oz.) can frozen orange juice concentrate, thawed
¾ c. sugar
¾ c. light corn syrup

Mix orange juice concentrate and sugar together in small saucepan. Heat over medium heat about 2 minutes, or until mixture starts to boil and sugar dissolves. Remove from heat. Add corn syrup; blend well. Serve warm or cooled on ice cream or cake. Store in covered container in refrigerator. Sauce may be reheated over low heat. Makes about 1¾ cups.

## PEACH AND NUT CONSERVE

*This luscious conserve is the perfect dress-up for plain ice cream*

6 c. chopped peeled peaches
Juice of 2 lemons
25 maraschino cherries, cut in
   quarters
3¾ c. sugar
1¼ c. chopped walnuts

Combine peaches, lemon juice, cherries and sugar in heavy preserving kettle; cook, stirring frequently, until thick, about 30 minutes. Add nuts and stir in well.

Ladle into hot, sterilized canning jars, filling to top of jars. Seal immediately. Makes 3 pints.

## SPICY CHERRY GLAZE

*For a showy dessert spoon glaze on a whole angel food or chiffon cake*

1½ c. drained, pitted tart
   canned cherries, 1 (16 to 17
   oz.) can
Juice drained from cherries
8 whole cloves
3 sticks cinnamon
2 tblsp. cornstarch
¼ c. sugar
¼ tsp. salt
⅓ c. light corn syrup
1 tblsp. butter
Red food color

Combine cherries, ½ c. cherry juice and spices in a saucepan. Bring to a boil. Reduce heat; simmer 5 minutes.

Stir together cornstarch, sugar and salt. Stir in 2 tblsp. cold cherry juice and corn syrup. Gradually stir in the hot liquid drained from the heated cherries. Remove whole spices from cherries; pour cornstarch mixture over cherries in saucepan. Cook, stirring frequently, over low heat until mixture thickens. Reduce heat and simmer 5 minutes. Remove from heat and stir in butter and enough food color to make sauce a regal red.

Cool slightly. Spoon over a 10″ angel food cake. Let glaze set about 2 hours before cutting. Makes 2 cups sauce.

NOTE: If you use sweetened frozen cherries, use 2 tblsp. sugar in making sauce instead of ¼ c.

## CHERRY/ALMOND SAUCE

*Red-black cherries, almonds and lemon peel blend flavors*

2 (1 lb. 1 oz.) cans pitted dark sweet cherries
2 c. cherry juice and water
2 tblsp. cornstarch
¼ c. sugar
¾ c. whole almonds, toasted
1 tsp. grated lemon peel

Drain cherries, reserving juice. To cherry juice, add water to make 2 cups.

Blend cornstarch and sugar in a saucepan; gradually add cherry juice. Cook over medium heat until mixture thickens, stirring frequently. Remove sauce from heat.

Meanwhile stuff each cherry with an almond. Stir lemon peel into sauce; add the stuffed cherries. Serve while warm. Makes 4 cups, about 16 average-size spoon-on toppings.

## CRANBERRY TOPPING

*An eye-catcher—gives plain cake a fancy look, adds vivid color*

1 c. heavy cream, whipped
½ c. sugar
1 (8½ oz.) can crushed pineapple, drained
1½ c. Cranberry Relish, partly thawed and drained (recipe follows)

Whip cream, adding sugar slowly, until stiff.

Fold in pineapple and relish, but do not blend completely. Serve on angel food cake slices or use as filling and topping for angel food and other cakes. Refrigerate frosted cakes until served. Makes about 1 quart.

## CRANBERRY RELISH

*Serve bright red cranberry sundaes with fingers of chiffon cake*

4 medium oranges
2 lbs. cranberries
2 medium unpeeled apples,
    cored

4 c. sugar

Take yellow peel from oranges; trim off and discard white part. Put orange pulp and peel, cranberries and apples through food chopper. Add sugar and mix well.

Pour into glass jars, leaving ½" head space. Seal and freeze. (Or cover and refrigerate but use relish within two weeks.) Makes 4 pints.

## PINK PARTY TOPPING

*Pretty pink sauce on white cake makes a festive dessert*

1 c. miniature marshmallows
1 (10 oz.) pkg. frozen red raspberries or strawberries
1 c. heavy cream, whipped

Pour marshmallows and frozen berries in a bowl. Cover; refrigerate overnight. Before serving, fold in whipped cream. Makes 3 cups.

## CHAPTER 6

# *Everyday Cakes the Family Will Love*

One of the favorite ways of serving homemade ice cream is over cake, still faintly warm. The men in the family especially relish a big wedge of cake topped with a large scoop of ice cream.

As cake bakers, farm women have a richly deserved reputation; they have collected blue ribbons at state and county fairs for their cakes for years. We have tested hundreds of them in our Countryside Test Kitchens. In this chapter we are featuring the down-to-earth cakes for everyday eating. Any one of them becomes a company dessert when topped with ice cream. They are versatile cakes—a spicy prune cake and a jiffy banana, perfect for packed lunches. There's a section on upside-down cakes and gingerbreads. For pound cake fanciers, we have chocolate, coconut, brown sugar and the traditional Southern.

Do try our Chocolate Walnut Loaf cut into slices topped with a scoop of ice cream and a drizzle of hot fudge sauce—a de luxe dessert. Serve the Squash Spice Cake à la mode and add a ladling of warm applesauce on a blustery winter night.

Many farm homemakers have developed delicious ways to add ingredients to today's cake mixes that make them taste almost as good as homemade.

Whether you serve these cakes with or without ice cream, you'll find the entire family will say, "Make this again, Mother."


## HOW TO BAKE A PERFECT CAKE EVERY TIME

Every woman wants to bake a superior cake and is dismayed when she takes a less-than-perfect result from the oven. Our Countryside Test Kitchen's staff is accustomed to questions like: Why is my cake bumpy with a big crack down the center? Why are my layer tops uneven in color instead of a perfect golden brown? What makes a cake dry as sawdust and coarse?

Actually, anyone can bake a perfect cake by following a few basic rules. Read the recipe. Follow the directions carefully. Measure ingredients accurately. Use the pan size specified in the recipe. Check oven temperature for accuracy.

## INGREDIENTS

The very first step in successful cake making is to measure ingredients accurately, using standard size measuring cups and measuring spoons.

**Flour:** We use all-purpose flour in our recipes unless we have specified another type. When a recipe calls for sifted flour, we sift the flour and then lightly spoon it into a measuring cup and level it off with the straight edge of a knife or spatula. Some women gently stir the flour in the canister to incorporate air, then lightly spoon it in the cup and level off. This they feel substitutes for sifting; however, we recommend always sifting and then you're sure to have an accurate measure.

**Leavening:** There are 3 leavening agents used in cake making. They are baking powder, baking soda and air. Sponge and angel cakes are leavened by the air that is incorporated into them during the beating period and by the steam that is created during the baking period. Butter cakes are leavened by baking powder or baking soda or in some cases by both.

**Fats:** The fats used in making the cakes in this book are butter, margarine (in sticks), lard, shortening, and vegetable salad oil. Soft tub-type margarines are whipped and contain air and less fat than the regular margarines. For best results, use the fat called for in the specific recipe. You can, however, substitute shortening for half the butter, if desired.

Pack solid fats firmly in measuring cup and level off. Be sure that the fat is at room temperature before you begin to make your cake.

**Sugar:** Use granulated white sugar unless otherwise specified. When a recipe calls for brown sugar, use light brown unless dark brown is specified. Superfine sugar is very fine granulated sugar, and we specify when it is to be used.

**Eggs:** We used large-sized eggs in our cake testing. If you have small eggs, try two of them in a ¼-cup measure (a large egg measures about ¼ cup).

**Milk and Cream:** When the recipe specifies sweetened condensed milk, be sure that is what you have (evaporated milk and sweetened condensed milk both come in cans; they cannot be used interchangeably). If you wish you can substitute evaporated milk for fresh milk if you mix it with an equal amount of water. Recipes designating buttermilk as an ingredient were tested with the commercial cultured type.

When a recipe calls for sour milk and you have none on hand, measure 1 tsp. vinegar or fresh lemon juice in a ¼-cup measure and fill with milk. Let stand a few minutes; then stir and use. For 1 cup sour milk, use 1 tblsp. vinegar or fresh lemon juice in a 1-cup measure.

Cream used in our recipes is either heavy or whipping (30 to 35% butterfat), coffee or light (18 to 20% butterfat), dairy half-and-half (10 to 12% butterfat) or dairy sour cream (commercial with 20% butterfat). Do not substitute one kind for another.

**Chocolate:** Recipes in this book call for one of four kinds of chocolate: unsweetened, semisweet, sweet cooking and no-melt un-sweetened in envelopes. *Use the specified type in each recipe.* You can substitute unsweetened chocolate squares for no-melt chocolate when recipe states it may be done. Melt the squares in a heavy bowl set in a pan of hot, not boiling water, or put the chocolate in the top of a double boiler over hot water. Chocolate can be melted in a small pan over very low direct heat, stirring constantly, but do watch it closely for chocolate scorches easily. Be sure to cool the melted chocolate before adding it to other ingredients.

## CAKE PANS

Be sure to use the size cake pan specified in the recipe; you want your baked cake to fill the pan but not bulge at the rim. Be sure, too, that your metal cake pans are shiny so that the cake will brown evenly. If you're using oven-glass cake dishes and you find that your cakes are too brown, try reducing the oven temperature 25°.

Before you start to mix your cake, prepare the pans, as the recipe directs.

## OVEN

If possible place the cake pan in the exact center of the oven to obtain the most uniform distribution of heat. If several cake layers are to be baked at the same time, place them in the oven so that they do not touch each other or the oven wall; the heat must circulate evenly around the pans. When staggering pans on two shelves in the oven, be sure not to place one pan directly under another.

Always preheat the oven. Check the accuracy of your temperature control from time to time for too low a temperature often produces a cake with poor volume, dry texture and sunken center. Too high a temperature can cause a cracked top, hard tough crust and a solid unpleasant texture.

Test the cake for doneness with a clean cake tester inserted in the center of the cake. If it comes out clean and dry, the cake is done. Underbaked cakes often have a sticky crust and doughy texture with a soggy layer near the bottom.

## COOLING CAKES

Butter cakes should be allowed to stand in the pan on a wire rack for about 5 minutes. Then remove from pan to cool, right side up on a wire rack. Sponge or angel food cakes, however, should be inverted and completely cooled in the pan. These cakes are so delicate that they cannot support their own weight in a high tube pan and must be allowed to hang inverted in the pan until thoroughly cooled. When the cake is completely cooled, loosen carefully from the pan with a spatula and turn out.

## SPICE SPECIALTIES

When days begin to be cool and you can hear the scrunch of fall leaves underfoot, it's time to bake your favorite spice cake. Here are some of our best spice cakes from farm kitchens.

## PRUNE SPICE CAKE

*A wonderful sugar 'n spice cake the whole family will go for*

| | |
|---|---|
| 1 c. boiling water | 1 tsp. ground cinnamon |
| 1 c. uncooked prunes, pitted and cut up | 1 tsp. ground nutmeg |
| | 1 tsp. ground cloves |
| 2 c. sifted flour | ½ c. salad oil |
| 1½ c. sugar | 3 eggs |
| 1 tsp. salt | 1 c. chopped nuts |
| 1¼ tsp. baking soda | Streusel Topping (recipe follows) |

Pour boiling water over prunes; let stand 2 hours.

Sift dry ingredients into large mixing bowl. Add prune mixture, oil, eggs and nuts. Blend thoroughly, about 1 minute. Beat 2 minutes at medium speed on mixer.

Pour into a greased and floured 13×9×2" pan. Sprinkle batter with Streusel Topping.

Bake in moderate oven (350°) 45 to 50 minutes. Cut in squares, serve warm. Makes 12 servings.

**Streusel Topping:** Mix ½ c. sugar, 2 tblsp. flour and 2 tblsp. soft butter or margarine until crumbly.

N O T E : You can bake batter in paper-lined muffin-pan cups 20 to 25 minutes. Omit Streusel Topping if you wish, and frost. Makes 12 cupcakes. Or bake in two 9" round layer cake pans 35 to 40 minutes. Delicious when cut in wedges and served hot with caramel sauce or vanilla ice cream.


## GLAZED PRUNE CAKE

*Everyone will want second helpings of this shiny glazed cake*

| | |
|---|---|
| 1 c. salad oil | 1 tsp. ground cinnamon |
| 1½ c. sugar | 1 tsp. ground nutmeg |
| 3 eggs | 1 tsp. ground allspice |
| 2 c. sifted flour | 1 c. cooked and mashed prunes |
| ½ tsp. salt | 1 c. buttermilk |
| 1 tsp. baking powder | 1 c. chopped pecans |
| 1 tsp. baking soda | Caramel Glaze (recipe follows) |

Cream oil and sugar. Add eggs one at a time, beating well after each addition.

Sift together dry ingredients. Add alternately to creamed mixture with prunes and buttermilk. Stir in pecans.

Pour into greased and floured 13×9×2" pan. Bake in moderate oven (350°) 35 minutes. Put pan on rack. Pour hot Caramel Glaze over cake immediately. Cool well. Makes 10 to 12 servings.

**Caramel Glaze:** Combine 1 c. sugar, ½ c. buttermilk, ½ tsp. baking soda, 1 tblsp. light corn syrup, ½ c. butter and ½ tsp. vanilla in medium saucepan. Bring to a rolling boil over low heat and boil 10 minutes, stirring occasionally.

## SQUASH SPICE CAKE

*Try a touch of apple cider in your favorite butter frosting*

½ c. butter or regular
  margarine

1½ c. brown sugar, firmly
  packed

2 eggs

2 c. sifted flour

¼ tsp. baking soda

2 tsp. baking powder

½ tsp. ground nutmeg

½ tsp. ground cinnamon

½ tsp. salt

¼ tsp. ground cloves

¼ c. buttermilk

¾ c. thick, sieved, cooked
  squash

½ c. chopped nuts

½ c. currants

Cream butter and brown sugar. Add eggs, one at a time; beat until light.

Sift together dry ingredients; add to creamed mixture alternately with buttermilk and squash; beat well after each addition. Add nuts and currants with last portion of flour; mix well.

Pour batter into two greased 8" round layer pans. Bake in moderate oven (350°) 25 to 30 minutes. Makes 10 servings.

## CIDER AND SPICE CAKE

*Grandmother called it October cake, but today folks call it* good!

3 c. sifted cake flour
1 tblsp. baking powder
¾ tsp. salt
1 tsp. ground cinnamon
1 tsp. ground nutmeg
¼ tsp. ground cloves
¾ c. shortening
1½ c. brown sugar, firmly
  packed

3 eggs, beaten
1 tblsp. lemon juice
1 c. apple cider
Cider Filling (recipe follows)
Creamy Cider Icing (recipe
  follows)

Sift together flour, baking powder, salt and spices.

Cream shortening and sugar; add eggs; beat until thoroughly blended.

Add lemon juice to cider. Add alternately with dry ingredients to creamed mixture, beating after each addition.

Pour batter into 3 greased 8″ round layer cake pans. Bake in moderate oven (350°) 25 to 30 minutes.

Let stand 10 minutes; turn out on racks to cool. Spread Cider Filling between layers; frost with Creamy Cider Icing. Makes 10 to 12 servings.

**Cider Filling:** Combine ½ c. sugar, ¼ tsp. salt and 3 tblsp. cornstarch in saucepan. Add 1 c. cider; mix. Cook over low heat, stirring constantly, until thick and clear. Remove from heat. Add 2 tblsp. lemon juice and 2 tblsp. butter or regular margarine. Cool.

**Creamy Cider Icing:** Melt ½ c. butter or regular margarine in saucepan; blend in 3½ tblsp. flour and ¼ tsp. salt. Add ½ c. cider; stir well. Bring to boil; cook 1 minute, stirring constantly. Remove from heat. Add 3 c. sifted confectioners sugar and beat well. Add ½ c. finely chopped nuts.

## CLOVE CAKE

*Garnish with a wreath of chopped walnuts for a pretty effect*

⅔ c. dairy sour cream
⅓ c. water
1 c. brown sugar, firmly packed
1 egg
1 tsp. lemon extract
1¼ c. sifted flour

1 tsp. baking soda
1 tsp. ground cinnamon
1 tsp. ground cloves
½ tsp. ground nutmeg
Cream Cheese Butter Frosting
    (recipe follows)

Combine sour cream and water; mix well. Gradually add brown sugar, beating well. Add egg and lemon extract; beat to mix well.

Sift together flour, baking soda and spices. Add to beaten mixture. Turn into greased 8″ square pan. Bake in moderate oven (350°) 25 to 30 minutes, or until cake tests done. Cool on rack. Frost with Cream Cheese Butter Frosting. Makes 9 servings.

**Cream Cheese Butter Frosting:** Whip together ⅓ c. butter, 1 (3 oz.) pkg. softened cream cheese, ½ tsp. lemon extract and 3 drops yellow food color. Add 2½ c. confectioners sugar and beat until light and fluffy. If mixture is too stiff, add a few drops milk to make frosting of spreading consistency.

# CHOCOLATE CAKES

Here's a grand variety of cakes for all those chocolate fans . . . a sheet cake spiced with cinnamon, a filled and frosted loaf, tender Chocolate Applesauce Cake and an extra-fudgy Chocolate Bark Cake.

## CHOCOLATE/CINNAMON SHEET CAKE

*A good, big cake to tote. Subtle taste of spice makes it different*

¼ c. cocoa
1 c. water
¾ c. shortening
2½ c. sifted flour
1 tsp. baking soda
1 tsp. salt
1 tsp. ground cinnamon

2 c. sugar
2 eggs
½ c. buttermilk
1 tsp. vanilla
Simple Chocolate Icing (recipe
    follows)

Mix cocoa and water in a saucepan; add shortening. Bring mixture to a boil. Cool slightly.

Sift together flour, baking soda, salt and cinnamon.

Blend together (do not beat) sugar and eggs in a large mixing bowl. Blend in cocoa mixture.

Add sifted dry ingredients alternately with buttermilk, stirring after each addition until well blended. Stir in vanilla.

Pour into greased 15½ × 10½ × 1" jelly roll pan. Bake in hot oven (400°) for 20 minutes. Cool on rack, then frost with Simple Chocolate Icing. Makes 18 servings.

**Simple Chocolate Icing:** Melt ½ c. butter or margarine in ¼ c. milk in small saucepan. Mix ¼ c. cocoa with 3 c. sifted confectioners sugar and stir into milk mixture. Add 1 tsp. vanilla. Spread on cake. Top with ½ c. chopped nuts.

## CHOCOLATE/HONEY LOAF

*Slices resemble ribbons—thin dark cake layers with creamy filling*

| | |
|---|---|
| 2 squares unsweetened chocolate | 1 tsp. vanilla |
| 1¼ c. sifted cake flour | ¼ c. sugar |
| ½ tsp. salt | ½ c. honey |
| ½ tsp. baking powder | 2 eggs |
| ¾ tsp. baking soda | ½ c. water |
| ⅓ c. butter or regular margarine | Honey/Pecan Filling (recipe follows) |
| | Chocolate Glaze (recipe follows) |

Melt chocolate; cool.

Sift together flour, salt, baking powder and soda.

Cream butter, vanilla and sugar. Gradually add honey, beating constantly until mixture is light and fluffy.

Add ¼ of flour mixture; beat thoroughly. Add eggs one at a time, beating well after each addition. Blend in chocolate.

Add remaining flour mixture alternately with water; beat thoroughly.

Grease sides of 15½ × 10½ × 1" jelly roll pan; line bottom with waxed paper. Pour batter evenly into pan. Bake in moderate oven (350°) 15 minutes or until done. Turn out of pan; remove paper and cool on rack.

Cut cake crosswise in half, then cut each half in half, making

4 oblong layers. Spread Honey/Pecan Filling between layers. Chill until firm.

Frost top and sides with Chocolate Glaze. With tip of spatula make pattern to decorate top. Refrigerate. Makes 12 servings.

**Honey/Pecan Filling:** Mix ¼ c. hot milk with 1 c. finely chopped pecans. Chill. Cream ½ c. butter or regular margarine. Add 1 egg yolk and ½ c. confectioners sugar; beat until thick and smooth. Gradually add ¼ c. honey, beating constantly (mixture should stay light and fluffy). Add nuts.

**Chocolate Glaze:** Melt 2 squares unsweetened chocolate and ¼ c. butter or regular margarine over low heat. Combine 2¼ c. sifted confectioners sugar, 3 tblsp. hot water, 1 tsp. vanilla and ⅛ tsp. salt. Add chocolate mixture. Beat with rotary beater until blended and thick but not stiff. Spread warm glaze on chilled cake.

## CHOCOLATE APPLESAUCE CAKE

*Serve this with mugs of steaming cocoa on a cold frosty day*

| | |
|---|---|
| 1 c. raisins | ½ tsp. ground cloves |
| ½ c. shortening | ½ tsp. ground nutmeg |
| 1 c. sugar | ½ tsp. ground allspice |
| 2 eggs | 3 tblsp. cocoa |
| 2 c. sifted flour | 1½ c. applesauce |
| 1½ tsp. baking soda | ½ c. chopped nuts |
| ½ tsp. salt | Cream Cheese Frosting (recipe |
| ½ tsp. ground cinnamon | follows) |

Cover raisins with water; let soak to plump.

Cream together shortening and sugar. Add eggs, beating well. Sift together flour, baking soda, salt, spices and cocoa. Add alternately with applesauce to creamed mixture, beating well. Stir in raisins and nuts. Pour into greased 13×9×2″ pan.

Bake in moderate oven (350°) 35 minutes. Cool on rack, then frost with Cream Cheese Frosting. Make 16 servings.

**Cream Cheese Frosting:** Combine 1 (3 oz.) pkg. softened cream cheese, 2¼ c. sifted confectioners sugar, ½ tsp. vanilla, dash of salt and 1 tsp. milk. Beat until smooth and of spreading consistency.

## CHOCOLATE BARK CAKE

*If you like chocolate fudge, this cake will rate high with you*

| | |
|---|---|
| 1½ c. boiling water | 6 tblsp. cocoa |
| 1 c. quick-cooking rolled oats | 1 tsp. baking soda |
| ¾ c. sugar | ½ tsp. salt |
| ½ c. brown sugar, firmly packed | 1 tsp. vanilla |
| ½ c. shortening | ¾ c. raisins |
| 2 eggs | ½ c. chopped nuts |
| 1 (6 oz.) pkg. semisweet | Chocolate Fudge Frosting |
| chocolate pieces, melted | (recipe follows) |
| 1½ c. sifted flour | |

Pour boiling water over oats; let stand.

Cream sugars and shortening thoroughly. Add eggs and beat well. Add chocolate.

Sift together flour, cocoa, baking soda and salt. Add alternately to creamed mixture with oats. Stir in vanilla, raisins and nuts. Spread in greased 13×9×2" pan.

Bake in moderate oven (350°) 35 to 40 minutes. Cool on rack, then frost with Chocolate Fudge Frosting. Mark surface of cake by running fork tines lengthwise on cake to look like the bark of a tree. Makes 12 to 16 servings.

**Chocolate Fudge Frosting:** In saucepan, combine 1½ c. sugar, 6 tblsp. butter and 6 tblsp. milk. Bring mixture to a boil, stirring constantly, and boil 1 minute. Remove from heat. Add ½ c. semisweet chocolate pieces. Cool slightly, then beat until thick and smooth.


# *WARM-FROM-THE-OVEN*
# *UPSIDE-DOWN CAKES*

Dish up any one of these succulent upside-down cakes and then top with a big scoop of vanilla ice cream. The ice cream melts and trickles through the fruit and cake . . . good eating!

## CHERRY UPSIDE-DOWN CAKE

*Delicious served warm—easy to fix when you have a busy day*

| | |
|---|---|
| 1 tblsp. butter | ¼ tsp. salt |
| 1 c. Frozen Cherry Mix (see Index) | ⅔ c. heavy cream |
| | 2 tblsp. milk |
| 1¼ c. sifted flour | ½ tsp. vanilla |
| ¾ c. sugar | 1 egg |
| 1½ tsp. baking powder | |

Melt butter in 8×8×2″ pan. Spread Cherry Mix evenly in pan. Sift dry ingredients together into mixer bowl. Add remaining ingredients. Mix to dampen dry ingredients. Beat 2 minutes at medium speed of electric mixer, or 300 vigorous strokes by hand.

Pour batter over Cherry Mix and spread evenly. Bake in moderate oven (350°) about 45 minutes, or until cake tests done. Remove from oven, let stand 5 minutes. Invert pan over cake plate, let stand 1 minute, then remove pan. Makes 9 servings.

## BLUEBERRY UPSIDE-DOWN CAKE

*Bake this cake on busy days—cake mix makes it a quickie dessert*

| | |
|---|---|
| ¼ c. butter or regular margarine | 1 tsp. grated lemon peel |
| | 1 (8½ oz.) pkg. yellow cake mix |
| ½ c. sugar | 1 tsp. grated lemon peel |
| 2 c. fresh or frozen unsweetened blueberries, thawed | ½ c. heavy cream, whipped (optional) |

Melt butter in 8″ square baking pan. Sprinkle sugar evenly over butter.

Mix blueberries and 1 tsp. lemon peel; sprinkle over sugar.

Prepare yellow cake mix according to package directions, stirring in 1 tsp. lemon peel at end of mixing. Spread batter over berries.

Bake in moderate oven (375°) for 30 minutes or until cake tests done. Let stand 10 minutes. Turn out on platter. Serve warm. Top with whipped cream at the table if you wish. Makes 9 servings.

## TOPSY-TURVY CAKE

*Let this dessert bake while everyone eats the main course*

| | |
|---|---|
| 1 (1 lb. 8 oz.) jar apple-pie filling | 1 tblsp. lemon juice |
| ½ tsp. ground cinnamon | 1 (18½ oz.) pkg. caramel or caramel-apple cake mix |
| ¼ tsp. ground nutmeg | ½ c. chopped nuts |
| ¼ tsp. ground ginger | Whipped cream |

Mix apple filling, spices and lemon juice. Pour into greased 13×9×2" pan.

Prepare batter as directed on package; add nuts. Pour over filling. Bake in moderate oven (350°) 30 minutes. Cut in squares. Serve warm, uspide down, with whipped cream. Makes 12 to 16 servings.

## UPSIDE-DOWN SWEET POTATO CAKE

*Spicy, moist gold cake to add to your recipe collection*

| | |
|---|---|
| 1 c. water | 1 c. chopped walnuts |
| 2½ c. sugar | 2½ c. sifted flour |
| 3 oranges, sliced ⅛" thick | 1 tblsp. baking powder |
| ¼ c. butter | ½ tsp. salt |
| ¼ c. brown sugar, firmly packed | 1 tsp. ground cinnamon |
| 1¼ c. lard | 1 tsp. ground nutmeg |
| 4 eggs, separated | ¼ c. milk |
| 1 tblsp. vanilla | Orange Sauce (recipe follows) |
| 1½ c. grated raw sweet potatoes | |

Bring water and ¼ c. sugar to a boil. Add orange slices. Cover and cook over medium heat 20 minutes. Drain, reserving liquid for sauce. Cool. Cut each orange slice in half.

Melt butter in 13×9×2" pan. Add ¼ c. sugar and brown sugar; spread mixture evenly over the pan. Arrange orange slices in 3 rows lengthwise in the pan.

Cream lard and the remaining 2 c. sugar until light. Beat in egg yolks; add vanilla and continue beating until fluffy; stir in potatoes and nuts.

Sift together flour, baking powder, salt, cinnamon and nutmeg;

add alternately with milk to creamed mixture. Beat egg whites until stiff and fold into creamed mixture. Spoon evenly over the orange slices in the pan.

Bake in a slow oven (325°) 1 hour. Cool in pan on rack 5 minutes; then invert on large plate or baking sheet. Serve warm with Orange Sauce. (Cake freezes well; wrap in foil and reheat to serve.) Makes 12 servings.

**Orange Sauce:** Add water to reserved orange liquid to make 1 c. Blend in 1 tblsp. cornstarch. Add ¼ c. sugar and 2 tblsp. butter. Cook over medium heat, stirring constantly, until mixture thickens slightly. Serve warm over cake.

### APRICOT UPSIDE-DOWN CAKE

*Serve this gold cake topped with whipped cream to company*

| | |
|---|---|
| ⅓ c. butter | 1 c. sugar |
| ½ c. brown sugar, firmly packed | 2 tsp. baking powder |
| | ½ tsp. salt |
| 3 tblsp. apricot juice | ⅓ c. shortening |
| 3 tblsp. light corn syrup | ⅔ c. milk |
| 30 dried apricots, cooked tender | 1 tsp. vanilla |
| 1⅓ c. sifted flour | 1 egg |

Melt butter in 9″ square pan; sprinkle on brown sugar, add apricot juice and corn syrup. Arrange apricots in pan.

Sift together flour, sugar, baking powder and salt. Add shortening, milk and vanilla. Beat about 2 minutes; add egg and beat 2 minutes longer. Pour over apricots in pan.

Bake in moderate oven (350°) 40 to 50 minutes, or until toothpick inserted in center of cake comes out clean. Immediately turn cake upside down on serving plate. Makes 8 servings.

## GINGERBREADS

Gingerbread is a top favorite with children and adults. Tuck a generous square in a lunch box for a treat. Good for field lunches and don't forget after-school snacks . . . serve warm with tall glasses of nourishing milk.

## GINGERBREAD DE LUXE

*This is an all-time favorite of our taste-testers—it's extra good*

| | |
|---|---|
| 2 c. sifted flour | ½ c. shortening |
| ¾ tsp. salt | ⅔ c. sugar |
| 2 tsp. baking powder | 2 eggs |
| ¼ tsp. baking soda | ⅔ c. light or dark molasses |
| ¾ to 1 tsp. ground ginger | ¾ c. boiling water |
| ¾ tsp. ground cinnamon | 1 c. heavy cream, whipped |
| ⅛ tsp. ground cloves | |

Sift together flour, salt, baking powder, soda and spices.

Cream together shortening and sugar. Beat in eggs, one at a time.

Gradually add molasses, beating constantly. Scrape beaters and sides of bowl.

Blend in dry ingredients, using low speed on mixer. Add water; mix until smooth.

Pour into well-greased and floured 8 or 9″ square pan. Bake in moderate oven (350°) 35 to 45 minutes.

Serve warm, topped with whipped cream. Makes 9 servings.

## WHOLE WHEAT GINGERBREAD

*Cake has nuts, raisins, candied lemon peel; it's spicy, not too sweet*

| | |
|---|---|
| ½ c. butter or regular margarine | ½ tsp. ground cinnamon |
| 2 tblsp. sugar | ½ tsp. ground mace or nutmeg |
| ¾ c. light molasses | ½ c. chopped walnuts |
| 1 c. sifted flour | ½ c. raisins |
| 1 c. stirred whole wheat flour | 3 tblsp. minced candied lemon peel |
| ½ tsp. salt | 2 eggs |
| ¾ tsp. baking soda | ½ c. milk |
| 1 tsp. ground ginger | |

Melt butter in a saucepan. Add sugar and molasses; stir to blend.

Sift together the dry ingredients into a large mixing bowl (include chaff from whole wheat flour). Stir in nuts, raisins and lemon peel.

Beat eggs and milk together and add to dry ingredients along with molasses mixture. Stir to moisten. Then beat mixture with a wooden spoon for about 70 strokes. Turn into a greased 8″ square baking pan.

Bake in moderate oven (350°) for 40 minutes or until cake tests done. Serve warm or cool on rack. Makes 10 servings.

## SPICY GINGERBREAD SQUARES

*A long-keeper. Serve warm or cold with a hot lemon sauce*

| | |
|---|---|
| 2 c. sifted flour | 1 tsp. ground allspice |
| ½ c. sugar | 1 tblsp. grated orange peel |
| ½ tsp. salt | 3 eggs |
| 1 tsp. baking soda | ½ c. light molasses |
| 2 tsp. ground ginger | 1 c. buttermilk |
| 1½ tsp. ground cardamom | ½ c. melted butter |

Sift together the dry ingredients into a large mixing bowl. Stir in orange peel.

In a separate bowl, beat eggs until thick, light and foamy. Add molasses in a stream, beating constantly. Gradually beat in buttermilk.

Add half of buttermilk-molasses mixture to dry ingredients. Beat with a spoon until well blended. Add remaining buttermilk-molasses mixture in two parts, beating well after each addition until well blended.

Gradually add butter and beat with spoon until batter is blended and smooth. Pour into greased 8″ square baking pan.

Bake in moderate oven (350°) 45 to 50 minutes or until toothpick inserted in center comes out clean. Makes 9 servings.

## CREOLE GINGERBREAD

*Orange-flavored frosting blends perfectly with spicy gingerbread*

| | |
|---|---|
| ¾ c. shortening | 1½ tsp. ground ginger |
| ¾ c. sugar | 1 tsp. salt |
| 3 eggs | ¾ c. milk |
| ¾ c. molasses | 1 c. flaked coconut |
| 3 c. sifted flour | Orange/Cream Cheese |
| 1½ tsp. baking soda | Frosting (recipe follows) |

Cream together shortening and sugar; beat until fluffy. Beat in eggs, one at a time, beating well after each addition. Add molasses, and mix.

Sift together flour, baking soda, ginger and salt. Add alternately with milk to creamed mixture, beating until smooth after each addition. Stir in coconut.

Turn into a greased 13×9×2" pan. Bake in moderate oven (350°) 40 to 45 minutes or until cake tests done. Cool and frost with Orange/Cream Cheese Frosting. Makes 12 servings.

**Orange/Cream Cheese Frosting:** Beat 1 (8 oz.) pkg. cream cheese until smooth and creamy. Beat in ¼ c. confectioners sugar and 2 tblsp. orange marmalade.

## APPLE GINGERBREAD

*For a crowd stack two of these gingerbreads—a dramatic dessert*

| | |
|---|---|
| ½ c. whole bran cereal | ½ tsp. baking powder |
| ½ c. light molasses | ½ tsp. ground ginger |
| ¼ c. shortening | ¼ tsp. ground cloves |
| ¼ c. boiling water | ¼ tsp. salt |
| 1 egg | 6 c. thinly sliced peeled apple |
| 1 c. sifted flour | ¼ c. melted butter |
| ½ tsp. baking soda | ¼ c. light corn syrup |

Mix bran, molasses, shortening and water. Add egg, and beat with rotary beater; let stand 5 minutes.

Sift together flour, soda, baking powder, spices and salt; add to bran mixture and stir only until blended. Pour into greased 8" square pan. Bake in moderate oven (350°) 20 minutes.

Arrange apple slices in layers over top. Brush with mixture of butter and syrup. Bake 10 minutes longer, or until apples are tender.

Remove from oven, brush apples with milk and broil just a few minutes to brown edges of apple slices (for a change, sprinkle chopped walnuts over apple slices). Serve warm. Makes 12 servings.

## TOPPINGS FOR GINGERBREAD

### LEMON HARD SAUCE

*You'll like what the tangy taste of lemon does to gingerbread*

¼ c. heavy cream
½ c. butter or regular
  margarine

1¼ c. confectioners sugar
1 tsp. grated lemon peel
1 tblsp. lemon juice

Whip cream; set aside.

Cream butter with same beaters. Add confectioners sugar; beat until light and fluffy. Add lemon peel and juice.

Fold in whipped cream. Chill. Serve spoonful on each square of gingerbread. Makes 2 cups.

### APPLESAUCE AND ICE CREAM

*Quick dessert if you have applesauce and ice cream on hand*

2 to 3 c. applesauce
1 to 2 pts. ice cream
Ground cinnamon

Top each serving of gingerbread with applesauce, then with a scoop of ice cream. Sprinkle with cinnamon.

### BANANA/CREAM TOPPING

*Bananas and gingerbread—a favorite for those cool autumn days*

1 (3 oz.) pkg. cream cheese
½ c. heavy cream
3 tblsp. sugar

Dash of salt
2 large ripe bananas
2 tsp. lemon juice

Beat cream cheese until smooth. Gradually add cream, beating only to keep mixture smooth. Add sugar and salt.

Mash bananas with fork; add with lemon juice to creamed mixture. Blend thoroughly. Cover and refrigerate. Makes 2 cups. (Use within 2 or 3 hours.)

## ORANGE/MARSHMALLOW SAUCE

*This fluffy sauce makes homemade gingerbread a company special*

| | |
|---|---|
| 4 c. miniature marshmallows | 1¼ c. orange juice |
| ½ c. water | 2 tblsp. lemon juice |
| 2 to 3 tsp. orange peel | Dash of salt |

Heat marshmallows and water to boiling in small saucepan. Remove from heat; stir to melt marshmallows.

Add peel, juices and salt. Chill until mixture congeals.

Beat with rotary beater until airy and light. Chill. Makes 2¼ cups.

## FRUIT AND HONEY CREAM

*Try your favorite canned fruit to top this, or diced, fresh pears*

1 c. heavy cream, whipped
¼ c. honey
1½ to 2 c. drained fruit cocktail

Top each gingerbread serving generously with whipped cream. Drizzle on about 1 tsp. honey; add spoonful fruit cocktail.

# LOAF CAKES

These are just right to bake and wrap in foil for your next bake sale or bazaar. All freeze well. Why not make one of each flavor and you'll be ready for drop-in guests? Cut into thin slices and top with your favorite ice cream.

## WHITE LOAF CAKE

*This versatile white cake is perfect with strawberries and cream*

| | |
|---|---|
| 1 c. butter | 1 c. milk |
| 1 c. sugar | 1 tsp. vanilla |
| 3½ c. sifted flour | 1 tsp. orange extract |
| 4 tsp. baking powder | 6 egg whites |
| ½ tsp. salt | 1 c. sugar |

Cream together butter and 1 c. sugar.

Sift together flour, baking powder and salt. Add to creamed mixture alternately with milk. Add vanilla and orange extract.

Beat egg whites until stiff. Slowly beat in 1 c. sugar. Fold into creamed mixture. Pour into 2 greased 9×5×3″ loaf pans.

Bake in slow oven (325°) 50 to 55 minutes, or until cakes test done. Cool on racks. Makes 2 loaves.

## CHOCOLATE/WALNUT LOAF

*Rich with chocolate, tender and moist—you'll enjoy every crumb*

| | |
|---|---|
| 1 c. butter or regular margarine | 1 tsp. vanilla |
| 2 c. sugar | 2½ c. sifted cake flour |
| 5 eggs, well beaten | 1 tsp. baking soda |
| 2 squares unsweetened chocolate, melted | ¼ tsp. salt |
| | 1 c. buttermilk |
| | 1 c. chopped walnuts |

Cream butter well, add sugar gradually. Beat until light and fluffy.

Add eggs and melted chocolate. Blend well. Add vanilla.

Sift together flour, baking soda and salt; add to creamed mixture alternately with buttermilk. Fold in nuts.

Pour batter in 2 greased 8½×4½×2½″ loaf pans. Bake in slow oven (325°) 1 hour.

Sprinkle top with confectioners sugar or spread with your favorite white or chocolate frosting. Makes 2 loaves.

## APPLESAUCE FIG LOAF

*Applesauce keeps this loaf moist—an all-time packed lunch favorite*

| | |
|---|---|
| ⅓ c. butter | ½ tsp. ground cinnamon |
| ⅔ c. sugar | ¼ tsp. ground nutmeg |
| 1 egg | 1 c. applesauce |
| 1 tsp. vanilla | 1 c. finely cut-up dried figs |
| 2 c. sifted flour | ½ c. chopped pecans |
| 1 tsp. baking powder | 1 tblsp. flour |
| 1 tsp. baking soda | |

Cream butter and sugar until fluffy. Add egg and vanilla; blend well.

Sift together flour, baking powder, soda and spices. Add to creamed mixture alternately with applesauce. Mix figs and nuts with 1 tblsp. flour and stir into batter.

Pour into greased 9×5×3″ loaf pan. Bake in moderate oven (350°) 50 minutes, or until cake tests done. Cool on rack. Makes 1 loaf.

## OLD-FASHIONED LEMON LOAF

*An old family favorite passed down through the generations*

| | |
|---|---|
| ⅓ c. butter | ½ c. milk |
| 1 c. sugar | 1 tsp. lemon extract |
| 2 eggs | 1 tsp. grated orange peel |
| 1½ c. sifted flour | ½ c. confectioners sugar |
| 1 tsp. baking powder | 1 tblsp. lemon juice |
| ½ tsp. salt | Chopped walnuts |

Cream together butter and sugar; add eggs and beat well.

Sift together flour, baking powder and salt. Add alternately with milk to creamed mixture. Stir in lemon extract and orange peel. Turn into a greased 9×5×3″ loaf pan. Bake in slow oven (325°) 45 minutes, or until cake tests done.

Meanwhile, make glaze by combining confectioners sugar and lemon juice.

Remove cake from oven and cool 5 minutes. Remove from pan and top with glaze, then sprinkle with nuts. Makes 1 loaf.

## PECAN GINGER LOAF

*Serve with a brick of softened cream cheese and fresh fruit*

| | |
|---|---|
| ½ c. soft butter or regular margarine | 2 tsp. ground ginger |
| | ½ tsp. ground cinnamon |
| 1½ c. sugar | ½ tsp. ground nutmeg |
| 2 eggs | ¼ tsp. ground cloves |
| 1⅔ c. unsifted flour | ⅓ c. water |
| ¾ tsp. salt | 1 c. cooked, mashed pumpkin |
| 1 tsp. baking soda | ½ c. finely chopped pecans |
| ¼ tsp. baking powder | |

Cream together butter and sugar with electric mixer. Add eggs, one at a time, and beat until mixture is light and fluffy.

Sift together the dry ingredients, add to creamed mixture alternately with water. Beat well after each addition. Add pumpkin and beat until well blended. Stir in chopped pecans. Turn into greased 9×5×3″ loaf pan and spread smooth.

Bake in moderate oven (350°) for 60 to 70 minutes, or until toothpick inserted in center comes out clean. Cool in pan for 10 minutes, then turn out on wire rack to cool thoroughly. Makes 1 loaf.

# LUNCH BOX SURPRISES

Everyone loves cupcakes. We have two party and two everyday recipes that are bound to please. The Black Bottom Cupcakes have a surprise in the center. They are elegant enough to serve to company.

## BLACK BOTTOM CUPCAKES

*The cream cheese and nut center is sure to please everybody*

| | |
|---|---|
| 2 (3 oz.) pkgs. cream cheese | 1 tsp. baking soda |
| 1 egg | ½ tsp. salt |
| ⅓ c. sugar | 1 c. water |
| ⅛ tsp. salt | ⅓ c. salad oil |
| 1 (6 oz.) pkg. semisweet | 1 tblsp. vinegar |
| chocolate pieces | 1 tsp. vanilla |
| 1½ c. sifted flour | 2 tblsp. sugar (optional) |
| 1 c. sugar | ½ c. chopped walnuts (optional) |
| ¼ c. cocoa | |

Beat cream cheese. Add egg, ⅓ c. sugar and ⅛ tsp. salt; blend well. Stir in chocolate pieces; set mixture aside.

Sift together into large bowl flour, 1 c. sugar, cocoa, baking soda and ½ tsp. salt.

Combine water, salad oil, vinegar and vanilla. Combine dry ingredients and liquids; beat well. Pour into paper-lined medium muffin-pan cups, filling one third full. Top each with large teaspoonful of cheese mixture. Sprinkle with sugar and chopped nuts.

Bake in moderate oven (350°) 35 minutes, or until done. Makes 18 cupcakes.

## SPICY CUPCAKES

*Children will love these spicy cupcakes in their packed lunches*

| | |
|---|---|
| 1 c. sugar | 1 tsp. ground allspice |
| ½ c. butter | ¼ tsp. salt |
| ½ c. molasses | ½ c. cold coffee |
| 2 eggs | ½ tsp. vanilla |
| 2 c. sifted flour | ¼ c. seedless raisins |
| ½ tsp. baking soda | ¼ c. chopped pecans |
| 1 tsp. ground cinnamon | 1 tblsp. flour |
| ½ tsp. ground cloves | |

Cream together sugar and butter until light and fluffy. Add molasses and eggs, and beat well.

Sift together 2 c. flour, baking soda, spices and salt. Add to creamed mixture alternately with coffee, mixing well. Add vanilla.

Coat raisins and pecans with 1 tblsp. flour; stir into batter. Pour into paper-lined medium muffin-pan cups, filling two thirds full. Bake in moderate oven (375°) about 25 minutes, or until done. If you like, spread tops with your favorite frosting. Makes 18.

## CHOCO/APPLE CUPCAKES

*Delicious when served with caramel or fudge frosting*

| | |
|---|---|
| ½ c. shortening | 1 tsp. ground cinnamon |
| 1 c. sugar | ½ tsp. ground allspice |
| 1 egg | 1½ squares unsweetened |
| 1¾ c. sifted flour | chocolate, grated |
| 1 tsp. baking soda | 1¼ c. unsweetened applesauce |
| ½ tsp. salt | |

Cream shortening and sugar until light and fluffy. Add egg; beat well.

Sift dry ingredients together. Stir in grated chocolate. Add to creamed mixture alternately with applesauce, mixing after each addition.

Fill greased muffin-pan cups two thirds full. Bake in moderate oven (375°) 20 minutes. Makes 18.

## AMBROSIA CUPCAKES

*Dainty, pretty—the flavor is an orange and coconut combination*

1 (9¼ oz.) pkg. white cake mix
2 egg whites
½ c. orange juice (about)
1½ tsp. grated orange peel

Confectioners Sugar Frosting
(recipe follows)
Food colors
1 (3½ oz.) can flaked coconut

Prepare cake batter according to package directions, using orange juice instead of water and adding orange peel.

Half fill tiny (1¾") greased cupcake pans. Bake in moderate oven (350°) 15 to 20 minutes. Cool.

Divide Confectioners Sugar Frosting into thirds. Tint each with a little food color—red, green and yellow—to make pastel pink, green and yellow frosting. Dip tops of cupcakes in frosting. While still moist, sprinkle with coconut. Let frosting set before storing. Makes 28 cupcakes.

**Confectioners Sugar Frosting:** Cream together 1½ c. sifted confectioners sugar and 3 tblsp. butter. Blend in 2 tblsp. light cream to make frosting of spreading consistency.

# PUDDING CAKES

A sauce and cake combination that some folks call a pudding and others a cake, but it's a luscious combination. The batter rises to the top and the sauce sinks to the bottom. Ladle into dishes and add a spoonful of slightly melted ice cream. Everyone will all be back for seconds and maybe thirds!

## RHUBARB PUDDING CAKE

*Serve in dessert bowls. Pass a pitcher of cream to pour over*

4 c. diced fresh rhubarb
1 c. sugar
¾ c. water
¼ c. shortening
½ c. sugar
1 egg

½ tsp. vanilla
1 c. sifted flour
2 tsp. baking powder
¼ tsp. salt
½ c. milk

Cook rhubarb, 1 c. sugar and water until rhubarb is tender; keep hot.

Cream shortening and ½ c. sugar; beat in egg and vanilla. Sift together flour, baking powder and salt; add alternately with milk to creamed mixture.

Pour batter into greased 9″ square baking pan. Spoon hot rhubarb sauce over batter. Bake in moderate oven (350°) 40 minutes. Makes 9 servings.

## PUMPKIN PUDDING CAKE

*Wrap baked cake in foil and freeze. Reheat in foil before serving*

| | |
|---|---|
| 1⅔ c. sifted flour | ⅓ c. soft shortening |
| 1⅓ c. sugar | 1 c. cooked, mashed or canned |
| ¼ tsp. baking powder | pumpkin |
| 1 tsp. baking soda | ⅓ c. water |
| 1 tsp. salt | 1 egg |
| 1 tsp. ground cinnamon | ⅔ c. raisins |
| ¼ tsp. ground ginger | ⅓ c. walnuts or pecans |

Sift together dry ingredients into mixing bowl; add shortening, pumpkin and water. Beat 2 minutes on medium speed of electric mixer or until ingredients are all well mixed. Add egg, beat 2 minutes longer. Stir in raisins and nuts.

Pour into a 1½-qt. ring or Turk's head mold that has been well greased and lightly dusted with fine, dry bread crumbs. Bake in moderate oven (350°) about 45 minutes, or until cake tests done. Serve warm with whipped cream or lemon sauce. Makes 8 servings.

## DUTCH PLUM CAKE

*Serve this fruity pudding cake warm, topped with whipped cream*

| | |
|---|---|
| ¾ c. sugar | ¼ c. shortening |
| ¼ c. flour | 1 egg, beaten |
| ¼ c. butter or regular | ⅓ c. milk |
| margarine | 1 tblsp. melted butter or regular |
| 1½ c. sifted flour | margarine |
| 2 tsp. baking powder | 12 to 16 ripe prune plums |
| ½ tsp. salt | 1 tblsp. lemon juice |
| 6 tblsp. sugar | Sweetened whipped cream or |
| ½ tsp. grated lemon peel | ice cream |

Mix together ¾ c. sugar and ¼ c. flour. Cut in ¼ c. butter to make fine crumbs; set aside.

Sift together 1½ c. flour, baking powder, salt and 6 tblsp. sugar. Add lemon peel. Cut in shortening with pastry blender until mixture resembles coarse meal.

Add egg and milk; stir to just moisten dry ingredients. Spread dough evenly in greased 8″ square pan. Brush with melted butter.

Wash and dry plums. Cut in halves and remove pits. Press four rows of halves, skin side down, on batter; let overlap a little. Leave some space between rows. Number will depend on size of plums.

Sprinkle with lemon juice; then with reserved crumb mixture.

Bake in moderate oven (375°) 45 minutes. Serve warm. Makes 6 servings.

## CHOCOLATE PUDDING CAKE

*Syrup sinks to bottom and cocoa cake rises to top during baking*

| | |
|---|---|
| 1 c. sifted flour | ¾ c. milk |
| ¾ c. sugar | 1 tsp. vanilla |
| 1½ tblsp. cocoa | ¾ c. chopped nuts |
| 2 tsp. baking powder | ½ c. chocolate syrup |
| ½ tsp. salt | 1 c. hot water |
| 2 tblsp. melted butter | |

Sift together flour, sugar, cocoa, baking powder and salt. Add butter, milk, vanilla and nuts. Stir until well mixed. Pour into greased 8″ square baking pan.

Mix chocolate syrup and hot water. Pour over batter in pan.

Bake in moderate oven (350°) 35 minutes. Makes 9 servings.

# PRIZE POUND CAKES

We have selected the best of farm women's pound cakes. They come from all over the country and in a variety of flavors. All taste just fine with a gentle dusting of confectioners sugar but two are "fancied up" with glazes.

## CHOCOLATE POUND CAKE

*Moist tender pound cake. You'll like the delicate chocolate flavor*

| | |
|---|---|
| 2 c. sugar | 3 c. sifted flour |
| 1 c. butter or regular margarine | ½ tsp. baking soda |
| 4 eggs | 2 tsp. salt |
| 2 tsp. vanilla | 1 c. buttermilk |
| 1 (4 oz.) pkg. sweet cooking chocolate, melted | |

Cream together sugar and butter. Add eggs one at a time, beating well after each addition. Add vanilla and melted chocolate. Blend in thoroughly.

Sift together flour, soda and salt. Add alternately with buttermilk to creamed mixture. Pour batter into lightly greased and floured 10″ tube pan.

Bake in slow oven (300°) 1½ hours. When done, let stand 10 minutes in pan; then remove cake from pan to rack and cover loosely until cool. Makes 16 servings.


## WALNUT POUND CAKE

*Wrap cake slices in foil and freeze. Handy to put in packed lunches*

| | |
|---|---|
| 1 lb. light brown sugar | ¼ tsp. salt |
| ½ c. sugar | 1 c. milk |
| 1½ c. butter | 2 tsp. vanilla |
| 5 eggs | 1 c. chopped walnuts |
| 3 c. sifted flour | 1 tblsp. flour |
| 1 tsp. baking powder | |

Cream together sugars and butter. Add eggs, one at a time, beating well after each addition.

Sift together 3 c. flour, baking powder and salt; add alternately with milk to creamed mixture. Add vanilla.

Combine walnuts with 1 tblsp. flour; stir into batter. Pour into greased and floured 10″ tube pan. Bake in slow oven (325°) 1½ hours, or until cake tests done. Cool on rack. Makes 10 to 12 servings.

## COCONUT POUND CAKE

*Make this big cake when you expect guests—it serves 12 people*

| | |
|---|---|
| 1 c. butter | 1 c. milk |
| 2 c. sugar | 1 (3½ oz.) can flaked coconut |
| 5 eggs | (1⅓ c.) |
| 3 c. sifted flour | 1 tsp. lemon extract |
| ¼ tsp. salt | ½ tsp. vanilla |

Using medium speed, cream together butter and sugar until light and fluffy. Add eggs, one at a time, beating well after each addition (takes about 10 minutes).

Sift flour with salt; add alternately with milk to creamed mixture, beating after each addition. Add remaining ingredients. Pour into greased and floured 10″ tube pan.

Bake in slow oven (325°) 1 hour and 30 minutes, or until cake tests done. Cool 10 minutes, then remove from pan and complete cooling on rack. Makes 12 servings.

## MARBLED POUND CAKE

*Cocoa makes this rich, moist cake different—no frosting needed*

| | |
|---|---|
| 1¼ c. soft butter | ½ tsp. salt |
| 2½ c. sugar | 1 c. less 2 tblsp. milk |
| 5 eggs | 2 tsp. vanilla |
| 2½ c. sifted flour | ¼ c. cocoa, sifted |
| 1¼ tsp. baking powder | Confectioners sugar (for top) |

Cream butter; gradually add sugar and beat until light and fluffy. Beat in eggs, one at a time, creaming well after each addition.

Sift together flour, baking powder and salt. Add alternately with milk and vanilla to creamed mixture.

Take out 2 c. cake batter and blend the cocoa into it. Alternately spoon the light and chocolate batters into a lightly greased and floured 10″ tube pan or a 10″ cast aluminum bundt-cake pan.

Bake in slow oven (325°) 1 hour and 10 minutes for a 10″ tube pan, or 1 hour and 30 minutes for the heavier, bundt-cake pan, or until cake tests done.

Cool in pan about 10 minutes. Invert cake on wire rack and re-move the pan. Cool cake thoroughly. Sift on confectioners sugar. Makes 10 to 12 servings.

## POUND CAKE

*Moist cake with silky grain keeps old customers and wins new ones*

| | |
|---|---|
| 1 c. butter | 3 c. sifted flour |
| 2 c. sugar | ½ tsp. baking soda |
| 4 eggs, unbeaten | ½ tsp. baking powder |
| 1 tsp. vanilla | ¾ tsp. salt |
| 1 tsp. lemon extract | 1 c. buttermilk |

Cream butter and sugar thoroughly. Add eggs, one at a time. Beat at medium speed with electric mixer 2½ minutes. Add flavorings.

Sift dry ingredients together; add to creamed mixture alternately with buttermilk. Beat 3½ minutes at medium speed. Do not overbeat or cake will fall.

Place in greased 10×5×3″ loaf pan (may overflow smaller pan). Bake in slow oven (325°) 1 hour and 10 minutes, or until done. Makes 10 servings.

## POPPY SEED POUND CAKE

*An old country favorite dressed up with a tangy orange glaze*

| | |
|---|---|
| 1 tblsp. poppy seeds | 1 tsp. almond extract |
| ¼ c. milk | 1 tsp. lemon extract |
| 6 eggs, separated | ¼ tsp. baking soda |
| 1 c. butter | 3 c. sifted flour |
| 2½ c. sugar | 1 tsp. baking powder |
| 1 c. buttermilk | Orange Glaze (recipe follows) |

Soak poppy seeds in milk.

Beat egg whites until stiff; set aside.

Cream together egg yolks, butter and sugar until fluffy.

Combine buttermilk, milk with poppy seeds, almond and lemon extracts and baking soda.

Sift together flour and baking powder; add to creamed mixture alternately with buttermilk mixture. Fold in egg whites. Pour into greased and floured 10″ tube pan. Bake in moderate oven (350°) about 1 hour and 15 minutes.

Remove from oven and cool 5 minutes. Remove from pan and pour Orange Glaze over top. Makes 12 servings.

**Orange Glaze:** Combine 1½ c. confectioners sugar, 1 tsp. almond extract and ½ c. orange juice; beat until smooth and glossy.

# DRIED AND FRESH FRUIT FAVORITES

Rich, moist, sturdy cakes studded with dried fruits are a famous specialty of many farm cooks. They're the kind of cakes that men like. As one woman expressed it, "My husband likes a cake he can sink his teeth into." We have plenty of these hearty cakes in this chapter along with a scrumptious choice of cakes made with fresh fruits . . . banana, blueberry, and fresh apple.

## SAUCY PRUNE CAKE

*Top with a dollop of sweetened whipped cream for a special treat*

| | |
|---|---|
| 3 eggs | ½ tsp. ground allspice |
| 1½ c. sugar | 1 c. buttermilk |
| 1 c. salad oil | 1 tsp. vanilla |
| 2 c. sifted flour | 1 c. cut-up cooked prunes |
| 1½ tsp. baking soda | 1 c. chopped toasted pecans |
| 1 tsp. ground cinnamon | Prune Cake Sauce (recipe |
| 1 tsp. ground nutmeg | follows) |

Beat eggs until light and fluffy. Gradually add sugar, continuing to beat. Add salad oil, beating well.

Sift together flour, baking soda and spices. Add alternately with buttermilk to egg mixture, starting and ending with dry ingredients. Add vanilla, prunes and pecans.

Pour into greased 13×9×2″ pan. Bake in slow oven (300°) 45 to 50 minutes, or until done. Cool slightly, then spoon Prune Cake Sauce over top. Makes 12 servings.

**Prune Cake Sauce:** In a saucepan, combine 1 c. sugar, ½ c. buttermilk, ½ tsp. baking soda, 1 tblsp. honey, ⅓ c. butter and ½ tsp. vanilla. Bring to boil and boil 1 minute, stirring occasionally. Pour over hot cake.

## SPICY PRUNE CAKE

*A three-layered beauty guaranteed to become a family favorite*

| | |
|---|---|
| 1 c. shortening | 1 tsp. ground mace |
| 2 c. sugar | ½ c. prune juice from cooked |
| 4 eggs | prunes |
| 3¼ c. sifted flour | 1 c. buttermilk |
| 1 tsp. baking soda | 1 tsp. vanilla |
| 2 tsp. baking powder | 20 cut-up cooked prunes |
| 1 tsp. salt | Lemon/Cream Cheese Frosting |
| 1 tsp. ground cinnamon | (recipe follows) |

Cream together shortening and sugar until fluffy. Add eggs, one at a time, beating well after each addition.

Sift together flour, baking soda, baking powder, salt and spices; add alternately with prune juice and buttermilk to creamed mixture. Add vanilla and prunes.

Pour into 3 greased 9″ round layer cake pans. Bake in moderate over (350°) 25 minutes, or until cakes test done. Cool on racks. Spread Lemon/Cream Cheese Frosting between layers and frost sides and top of cake. Makes 12 servings.

**Lemon/Cream Cheese Frosting:** Combine ½ c. butter or regular margarine, 1 (8 oz.) pkg. cream cheese and 1 tsp. vanilla; cream well. Gradually add 1 lb. sifted confectioners sugar, 1 tsp. grated lemon peel and a few drops of yellow food color. Beat well, adding a little milk if necessary to make frosting of spreading consistency.

## HARVEST PRUNE CAKE

*A California prune grower's wife shares this treasured recipe*

| | |
|---|---|
| ½ c. shortening | ½ tsp. ground nutmeg |
| 1½ c. sugar | ⅛ tsp. ground cloves |
| 3 eggs | 2 tsp. ground cinnamon |
| 2¼ c. sifted flour | 1 c. liquid from cooked prunes |
| 1 tsp. baking powder | 1 tsp. vanilla |
| 1 tsp. salt | 1 c. chopped cooked prunes |
| ¾ tsp. baking soda | ½ c. chopped walnuts |

Cream shortening; add sugar and then eggs, one at a time, beating thoroughly.

Sift together flour, baking powder, salt, baking soda and spices. Blend into creamed mixture, alternately with prune liquid. Stir in vanilla, prunes and nuts.

Spread batter into greased 13×9×2″ pan. Bake in moderate oven (350°) 40 to 50 minutes, or until cake tests done in center.

Remove from oven; set pan on rack to cool 10 minutes. Loosen cake around edges with spatula and invert on rack, lift off pan and cool thoroughly. Serve plain, à la mode or spread with Cream Caramel or Caramel/Nut Frosting. Makes 16 servings.

## CREAM CARAMEL FROSTING

*Country hostesses make caramel frosting with cream. Guests approve*

| | |
|---|---|
| 1 c. sugar | ⅛ tsp. salt |
| 1 c. brown sugar, firmly packed | 1 tsp. vanilla |
| ⅔ c. sweet or dairy sour cream | |

Combine sugars, cream and salt in saucepan. Heat slowly, stirring until sugars dissolve. Cook without stirring to the soft ball stage (234°). Remove from heat. Cool without stirring until lukewarm.

Add vanilla and beat until thick and creamy. If necessary, thin frosting with a few drops of cream. Makes enough to frost a 13× 9×2″ cake.

## *Variation*

**Caramel/Nut Frosting:** Add ¼ c. chopped walnuts to frosting just before spreading it on the cake.

## RAISIN CAKE

*An old-fashioned, good-eating cake that your family will love*

| | |
|---|---|
| 2 c. sugar | 2 tsp. baking soda |
| 2 c. hot water | 3½ c. sifted flour |
| 1 c. shortening | ½ tsp. salt |
| 1 (1 lb.) pkg. raisins | Confectioners Sugar Frosting |
| 1 tsp. ground cinnamon | (recipe follows) |
| ½ tsp. ground cloves | |

Combine sugar, hot water, shortening, raisins and spices in a deep saucepan. Bring to a boil and boil 1 minute. Remove from heat. Add baking soda immediately; beat well. (Mixture will foam when baking soda is added.) Cool.

Sift together flour and salt; stir into cooled mixture and mix well. Pour into greased 13×9×2″ pan. Bake in moderate oven (350°) 1 hour, or until cake tests done. Cool on rack, then frost with Confectioners Sugar Frosting. Makes 12 servings.

**Confectioners Sugar Frosting:** Cream ¼ c. butter. Gradually beat in 2 c. sifted confectioners sugar, ½ tsp. vanilla, dash of salt and enough milk (2 to 2½ tblsp.) to make frosting of spreading consistency.

## DOUBLE DATE CAKE

*The luscious date filling helps to keep cake moist for several days*

| | |
|---|---|
| 1 c. chopped dates | 1¾ c. sifted flour |
| 1 tsp. baking soda | 1 tsp. baking powder |
| 1 c. boiling water | ½ c. chopped nuts |
| 1 c. sugar | 1 tsp. vanilla |
| 2 tblsp. butter | Date Topping (recipe follows) |
| 1 egg | |

Mix dates and baking soda. Add boiling water, and let stand.

Combine sugar, butter and egg; beat well. Stir in date mixture. Add flour, baking powder, nuts and vanilla. Mix well.

Pour into greased and floured 9×5×3″ loaf pan. Bake in moderate oven (350°) 45 to 50 minutes. Cool on rack. Spread cooled cake with Date Topping. Makes 1 loaf.

**Date Topping:** Combine 1 (8 oz.) pkg. dates, chopped, ½ c. sugar and ¾ c. water; cook until thick. Stir in ½ c. walnuts.

## DATE CAKE IRRESISTIBLE

*A moist rich cake—serve at dessert party with whipped cream*

| | |
|---|---|
| 1½ c. boiling water | 1 tsp. vanilla |
| 1 c. cut up pitted dates (½ lb.) | 1½ c. sifted flour |
| 1 tsp. baking soda | 1 c. sugar |
| ¼ c. butter or margarine | 1 tsp. baking powder |
| 1 egg, beaten | Date Topping (recipe follows) |
| ½ tsp. salt | |

Combine boiling water, dates, baking soda and butter. Set aside.

Combine egg, salt and vanilla; beat to mix. Sift together flour, sugar and baking powder. Alternately add dry ingredients with cooled date mixture to egg mixture, beating after each addition (batter is thin).

Bake in greased and paper-lined 13×9×2″ pan in moderate oven (350°) 35 to 40 minutes. Cool on rack. Spread with Date Topping. Makes 12 servings.

### Date Topping

1 c. cut up pitted dates (½ lb.)  
¾ c. water  
¾ c. sugar  
⅛ tsp. salt  
½ c. chopped walnuts or black walnuts

Combine all ingredients except nuts; cook until smooth, stirring constantly, about 10 minutes. Add nuts. Cool.

### POLKA DOT CAKE

*Good to serve at summer picnics—there's no frosting to melt*

1¼ c. chopped dates  
1 c. hot water  
¾ c. butter or regular margarine  
1 c. sugar  
2 eggs  
2 c. sifted flour  
1 tsp. baking soda  
½ tsp. salt  
1 tsp. vanilla  
1 (6 oz.) pkg. semisweet chocolate pieces  
½ c. chopped nuts

Mix chopped dates and hot water; set aside to cool.

Cream together butter and sugar. Add eggs; beat until fluffy.

Sift together flour, soda and salt. Add to creamed mixture alternately with date mixture. Mix well after each addition. Stir in vanilla and ½ c. chocolate pieces. Spread batter in greased 13×9×2″ baking pan.

Top with remaining chocolate pieces and the nuts. Bake in a moderate oven (350°) for about 35 minutes. Makes 15 servings.

## APPLESAUCE CAKE

*Good use for your extra apples—make applesauce for this cake*

⅔ c. butter or regular
  margarine
2 c. sugar
4 eggs, separated
¾ c. unsweetened applesauce
2½ c. cake flour
3 tsp. baking powder
1 tsp. ground cinnamon
½ tsp. ground cloves

½ tsp. ground nutmeg
1 tsp. salt
¼ c. cocoa
½ c. milk
1 tsp. vanilla
⅔ c. chopped plumped raisins
½ c. chopped nuts
Brown Sugar Frosting (recipe
  follows)

Cream together butter and sugar. Add egg yolks and applesauce; beat until smooth.

Sift together flour, baking powder, spices, salt and cocoa three times. Add to creamed mixture alternately with milk. Add vanilla, raisins and nuts.

Beat egg whites until stiff; fold into batter. Pour into 2 greased 9″ round layer cake pans. Bake in moderate oven (350°) 40 minutes, or until cake tests done. Cool on racks, then put layers together and frost with Brown Sugar Frosting. Makes 10 to 12 servings.

**Brown Sugar Frosting:** Melt ½ c. butter in saucepan. Stir in 1 c. brown sugar, firmly packed. Boil over low heat 2 minutes, stirring constantly. Stir in ¼ c. light cream; continue stirring constantly, and bring to a gentle boil. Remove from heat; cool to lukewarm. Gradually stir in 1¾ c. sifted confectioners sugar. Beat until thick and smooth. Add ½ tsp. vanilla. Let stand a few minutes, or until of spreading consistency.

## MARSHMALLOW/APPLESAUCE CAKE

*Push marshmallows into the batter . . . they rise to make the frosting*

| | |
|---|---|
| 2¾ c. unsifted flour | ½ tsp. ground allspice |
| 2 c. sugar | ½ c. soft shortening |
| 1½ tsp. baking soda | 2 eggs |
| 1½ tsp. salt | 2 c. unsweetened applesauce |
| ¼ tsp. baking powder | 1 c. walnut halves |
| 1 tsp. ground cinnamon | 20 large marshmallows (¼ lb.) |
| ½ tsp. ground cloves | |

Sift together flour, sugar, soda, salt, baking powder and spices. Add soft shortening, eggs and applesauce. Beat until smooth and well blended.

Stir in walnuts. Pour into greased and floured 13×9×2″ pan. Press whole marshmallows into batter to bottom of pan—in 4 rows, 5 in each row.

Bake in moderate oven (350°) about 50 minutes. Cool on rack. Makes 20 servings.

## FIRST PRIZE APPLESAUCE CAKE

*A hint of cocoa gives distinctive flavor to this winner*

| | |
|---|---|
| 4 c. sifted flour | 2 c. sugar |
| 4 tsp. baking soda | 3 c. unsweetened applesauce, |
| 1¼ tsp. salt | heated |
| 2 tsp. ground cinnamon | ½ c. raisins |
| ½ tsp. ground nutmeg | ½ c. chopped walnuts |
| ½ tsp. ground cloves | Caramel Frosting (recipe |
| 2 tblsp. cocoa | follows) |
| 1 c. salad oil | |

Sift together flour, soda, salt, spices and cocoa.

In a large mixing bowl combine oil and sugar. Beat until well blended. Stir in hot applesauce, blending thoroughly. Add dry ingredients, blending well. Stir in raisins and walnuts.

Turn batter into 2 well-greased and floured 9″ square cake pans. Bake in hot oven (400°) 15 minutes; then reduce oven temperature to moderate (375°) and bake about 15 minutes longer. Remove to racks. Let stand in pans 5 minutes. Remove from pans and complete cooling on racks. Fill and frost with Caramel Frosting. Makes 9 to 12 servings.

**Caramel Frosting:** Melt ½ c. butter in saucepan over low heat. Stir in 1 c. dark brown sugar, firmly packed, and ¼ tsp. salt. Bring to a boil over medium heat; boil hard 2 minutes, stirring constantly. Remove from heat. Stir in ¼ c. milk. Return pan to heat and bring to a full boil. Remove from heat, cool to lukewarm. Stir in 2 c. confectioners sugar and beat until smooth. If frosting is too thick, beat in a little milk.

## MAE'S FRESH APPLE CAKE

*A recipe you'll want to keep handy when green apples are plentiful*

| | |
|---|---|
| 1 c. butter or regular margarine | 1 tblsp. ground cinnamon |
| 2 c. sugar | 3½ c. finely chopped tart apples |
| 2 eggs | (about 12 small) |
| 1 tsp. vanilla | 1 c. chopped walnuts |
| 2 c. unsifted flour | Sifted confectioners sugar |
| 1½ tsp. baking soda | Brown Butter Frosting (recipe |
| 1 tsp. salt | follows) |

Cream butter and sugar thoroughly. Add eggs and vanilla; beat to mix.

Sift together flour, baking soda, salt and cinnamon; add to creamed mixture alternately with apples. Beat well. Add nuts, and beat again.

Pour into ungreased 13×9×2″ glass baking dish. Bake in moderate oven (350°) 45 to 55 minutes. Cool on rack, then sprinkle with confectioners sugar. Or, if you like, frost with Brown Butter Frosting. Makes 12 to 16 servings.

N O T E : If you bake cake in 13×9×2″ metal baking pan, increase oven temperature to 375°.

**Brown Butter Frosting:** Melt ⅓ c. butter over medium heat until delicate brown. Blend in 3 c. confectioners sugar. Stir in 1½ tsp. vanilla and enough milk (about 2 tblsp.) to make a frosting of spreading consistency.

## BANANA CAKE

*Add a sprinkling of chopped maraschino cherries for bright note*

3 large bananas, sliced
1 tsp. baking soda
1½ c. sugar
¾ c. salad oil
2 eggs

2 c. sifted flour
¼ tsp. salt
½ c. chopped nuts
Lemon Pudding Sauce (recipe
   follows)

Mix banana slices with baking soda; set aside.

Combine sugar and oil in mixing bowl. Add eggs, one at a time, beating after each addition.

Sift flour with salt; add to creamed mixture. Mix well. Stir in bananas and nuts. Turn into greased 10×7×2″ glass baking dish. Bake in moderate oven (350°) 45 to 50 minutes, or until cake tests done. Serve warm or cold with Lemon Pudding Sauce. Makes 8 servings.

**Lemon Pudding Sauce:** Prepare 1 (3½ oz.) pkg. lemon pudding and pie filling as directed on package, adding an additional ½ c. water.

## JIFFY BANANA CAKE

*Serve cake squares with steaming cups of hot chocolate for a break*

1 (17 to 18½ oz.) pkg. yellow
   cake mix
2 medium bananas

1 tblsp. lemon juice
3 tblsp. confectioners sugar

Bake cake according to directions on box. Use two 8″ round cake pans.

Slice bananas; mix with lemon juice.

Arrange bananas on one hot layer; sprinkle with sugar. Serve warm. Makes 4 to 6 servings. Freeze extra cake layer.

NOTE: To make a design on cake's top, fasten a small, plain paper doily with scalloped edges in center of cake with toothpick. Arrange banana slices around edge; sift sugar on fruit and cake. Remove doily.

## BLUEBERRY CAKE

*A favorite cake for family reunions and summer picnics*

| | |
|---|---|
| 1 c. shortening | ⅔ c. milk |
| 1½ c. sugar | ½ c. sugar |
| 2 tsp. vanilla | 3 c. blueberries (fresh, frozen |
| 4 eggs, separated |    or canned, drained) |
| 3 c. sifted flour | 1 tblsp. flour |
| 2 tsp. baking powder | Sifted confectioners sugar |
| ½ tsp. salt | |

Cream together shortening and 1½ c. sugar. Add vanilla and egg yolks; beat until light and fluffy.

Sift togther 3 c. flour, baking powder and salt. Add alternately to creamed mixture with milk.

Beat egg whites until stiff; gradually add ½ c. sugar. Fold into batter. Add blueberries mixed with 1 tblsp. flour. Pour into greased 13×9×2″ pan. Bake in moderate oven (350°) 50 minutes, or until cake tests done. When cool, sprinkle with confectioners sugar. Makes 12 servings.

## MARSHMALLOW/BANANA BARS

*These bars are great for outdoor eating: picnics and camping*

| | |
|---|---|
| 1½ c. sifted flour | 1 tsp. vanilla |
| 1 tsp. baking powder | 1⅓ c. mashed bananas |
| ½ c. shortening | 1 (7 oz.) jar marshmallow |
| 1 c. sugar |    creme |
| 1 egg | Vanilla Icing (recipe follows) |
| 1 tsp. baking soda dissolved | |
|    in 1 tblsp. water | |

Sift together flour and baking powder.

Cream shortening and sugar. Add egg; beat well. Stir in soda mixture and vanilla. Add dry ingredients alternately with bananas, beating well after each addition.

Spread into a greased 15½×10½×1″ jelly roll pan. Bake in moderate oven (350°) 25 to 30 minutes. Remove from oven. Drop spoonfuls of marshmallow creme on cake. Let stand 2 minutes. Spread gently over surface of cake. Cool; frost with vanilla icing. Cut in bars to serve. Makes 20 to 24 servings.

**Vanilla Icing:** Combine 2 c. sifted confectioners sugar, 1 tblsp. butter, 2 tblsp. milk, 1 tsp. vanilla and a few drops yellow food color. Blend until smooth.

### PINEAPPLE/NUT CAKE

*This attractive cake is perfect dusted with confectioners sugar*

| | |
|---|---|
| 3 c. sifted flour | 3 eggs |
| 1 tsp. baking soda | 2 c. grated carrots |
| 2 tsp. baking powder | ½ c. chopped walnuts |
| 2 tsp. ground cinnamon | 1 (8¼ oz.) can crushed |
| ½ tsp. salt | pineapple, undrained |
| 1 c. butter | 2 tsp. vanilla |
| 2 c. sugar | |

Sift together flour, baking soda, baking powder, cinnamon and salt.

Cream butter and sugar. Add eggs; beat until fluffy. Stir in dry ingredients, carrots, walnuts, pineapple and vanilla. Mix well.

Pour into greased 13×9×2″ pan. Bake in moderate oven (350°) 55 to 60 minutes, or until cake tests done. Cool on rack. Makes 12 servings.

## BAZAAR CAKES

Any one of these cakes will travel nicely to your next cake or bazaar sale and will disappear in a wink.

In fact, we suggest that you bake two and leave one at home for the family to enjoy. Keep these in mind, too, for family reunion or picnic gatherings as they are easy to tote as well as delicious to eat.

## BROWN MOUNTAIN CAKE

*Perfect for picnics—slices neatly, easy to tote, tastes wonderful*

| | |
|---|---|
| 1 c. soft butter | ½ tsp. salt |
| 2 c. sugar | 3 tblsp. cocoa |
| 3 eggs | 1 c. buttermilk |
| 3 c. sifted flour | 1 tsp. vanilla |
| 1 tsp. baking soda | ½ c. warm water |

Cream butter and sugar until light and fluffy. Beat in the eggs, one at a time. Sift together the flour, baking soda, salt and cocoa; add alternately with buttermilk to the creamed mixture. Stir in vanilla and warm water.

Pour batter into a lightly greased and floured 13×9×2" baking pan. Bake in moderate oven (350°) about 45 minutes, or until the cake tests done.

Cool cake on rack. Frost with your favorite chocolate frosting. Makes 16 servings.

N O T E : If you do not have buttermilk, use soured milk. Put 1 tblsp. vinegar into a 1-cup measuring cup and fill with sweet milk. Let stand a few minutes.

## CHOCOLATE DATE CAKE

*This is a marvelous cake to take to the field or tuck in lunch boxes*

| | |
|---|---|
| ¾ c. butter | 1 tsp. pumpkin pie spice |
| ¾ c. brown sugar, firmly packed | ½ tsp. salt |
| ¾ c. sugar | 1 c. chopped dates |
| 1⅓ c. unsweetened applesauce | 2 tsp. baking soda |
| 3 c. sifted flour | 1 c. sour milk |
| ¼ c. cocoa | |

Cream together butter and sugars until light and fluffy. Add applesauce; beat well.

Sift together flour, cocoa, pumpkin pie spice and salt. Remove ¼ c. flour mixture and mix with dates.

Combine baking soda with milk. Add dry ingredients to creamed mixture alternately with milk, beating well. Stir in dates.

Pour into greased and floured 13×9×2" cake pan. Bake in moderate oven (350°) for 45 minutes or until cake tests done. Makes 16 servings.

## CHOCOLATE CHIP DATE CAKE

*Youngsters will love the crunchy chocolate chip and nut topping*

1½ c. boiling water
1 c. chopped dates
1 tsp. baking soda
½ c. shortening
1 c. sugar
2 eggs
1¾ c. sifted flour

¼ tsp. salt
¾ tsp. baking soda
1 (6 oz.) pkg. semisweet
  chocolate pieces
½ c. sugar
½ c. chopped walnuts

Pour boiling water over dates and baking soda and allow to cool.

Cream together shortening and 1 c. sugar. Add eggs; beat until light and fluffy.

Sift together flour, salt and baking soda. Stir in date mixture and flour, mixing well.

Pour into greased 13×9×2″ cake pan. Combine chocolate chips, ½ c. sugar and chopped nuts. Sprinkle over cake batter.

Bake in moderate oven (350°) for 35 minutes or until cake tests done. Makes 16 servings.

## JAM-BAR CAKE

*You bake the cake batter on jam to make a ribbon cake layer*

¼ c. butter
1 c. red raspberry jam
4 eggs
¾ c. sugar

1 tsp. vanilla
¾ c. sifted cake flour
1 tsp. baking powder
1 tsp. salt

Melt butter in 15½×10½×1″ jelly roll pan. Mix jam with butter spread evenly over bottom of pan.

Beat eggs until thick and lemon-colored. Add sugar, 1 tblsp. at a time, beating after each addition. Add vanilla.

Sift together remaining dry ingredients and fold into egg mixture in 2 parts. Spread batter evenly over jam in pan. Bake in hot oven

(400°) 15 to 18 minutes. Remove from oven and let stand in pan for 5 minutes.

Then invert pan on sheet of wrapping paper or towel lightly dusted with confectioners sugar. Let stand 2 or 3 minutes. Then lift pan gradually, allowing cake to fall out slowly. Assist carefully with spatula, if necessary.

Cut cake crosswise in 2 equal pieces. Invert one piece over the other so that jam edges are together. Use paper to assist in turning one piece over the other. Cut in 2½×1½″ pieces. Makes 20.

N O T E : You can use strawberry, apricot or other jam instead of raspberry.

### DEAN'S SHEET CAKE

*A good cake to make when you expect a crowd—it serves 18*

| | |
|---|---|
| 1 c. butter or regular | 2 eggs |
| margarine | ½ c. dairy sour cream |
| 1 c. water | 1 tsp. baking soda |
| ¼ c. cocoa | Thin Cocoa Frosting (recipe |
| 2 c. flour | follows) |
| 2 c. sugar | |

Combine butter, water and cocoa in saucepan. Heat until butter is melted.

Sift flour and sugar into large mixing bowl; add butter mixture and mix well.

Combine eggs, sour cream and baking soda in small bowl; mix well. Add to flour mixture, mixing well. Pour batter into greased and floured 15½×10½×1″ jelly roll pan. Bake in hot oven (400°) 20 minutes, or until cake tests done. Cool on rack, then frost top of cake with Thin Cocoa Frosting. Makes 20 to 24 servings.

**Thin Cocoa Frosting:** Heat in small saucepan ¼ c. butter or regular margarine, 2 tsp. cocoa and 3 tblsp. milk until butter is melted. Remove from heat and add to 2⅓ c. sifted confectioners sugar, ½ tsp. vanilla and ⅛ tsp. salt in mixing bowl. Beat until frosting is of spreading consistency.

## CINNAMON COFFEE SQUARES

*Pass these subtly spiced treats with coffee next time you entertain*

3 c. sifted flour
2 tsp. baking powder
2 tsp. ground cinnamon
½ tsp. baking soda
½ tsp. salt

1 c. butter
2 c. brown sugar, firmly packed
2 eggs
1 c. hot coffee
Butter Icing (recipe follows)

Sift together flour, baking powder, cinnamon, soda and salt.

Cream together 1 c. butter, brown sugar and eggs until fluffy. Alternately add dry ingredients and coffee, beating after each addition.

Pour into greased 13×9×2″ baking pan. Bake in moderate oven (350°) 35 minutes, or until cake tests done. Cool. Makes 12 servings.

**Butter Icing:** Combine 2 c. sifted confectioners sugar, ⅓ c. butter, 1½ tsp. vanilla, dash of salt and 2 tblsp. milk. Blend until smooth.

## WALNUT WONDER CAKE

*This moist cake is so easy to make . . . needs no additional frosting*

1 c. shortening
1 c. sugar
2 eggs
1 tsp. vanilla
2 c. sifted flour
1 tsp. baking powder
1 tsp. baking soda

½ tsp. salt
1 c. dairy sour cream
⅓ c. brown sugar, firmly
  packed
¼ c. sugar
1 tsp. ground cinnamon
1 c. chopped walnuts

Cream together shortening and 1 c. sugar. Add eggs and vanilla; beat well.

Sift together flour, baking powder, soda and salt; add alternately with sour cream to creamed mixture.

In a separate bowl, blend together remaining ingredients to make a crumb mixture.

Pour half of cake batter into a greased 13×9×2″ pan. Sprinkle half of crumb mixture evenly over batter. Add remaining batter to pan; top with remaining crumb mixture. Bake in moderate oven (350°) about 35 minutes. Cool on rack. Makes 16 servings.

## ORANGE LARD CAKE

*Dress up this cake by sprinkling coconut on freshly spread frosting*

2 eggs, separated
½ c. sugar
⅓ c. lard
2¼ c. sifted cake flour
1 c. sugar
2½ tsp. baking powder
1 tsp. salt

¼ tsp. baking soda
¾ c. milk
⅓ c. orange juice, fresh or
reconstituted frozen
¼ tsp. almond extract
Orange Butter Cream Frosting
(recipe follows)

Beat egg whites until frothy. Gradually beat in ½ c. sugar. Continue beating until very stiff and glossy.

In another bowl stir lard to soften. Add sifted dry ingredients and milk. Beat 1 minute, medium speed on mixer. Scrape bottom and sides of bowl constantly.

Add orange juice, egg yolks and almond extract. Beat 1 minute longer, scraping bowl constantly.

Fold in egg white mixture.

Pour into 2 greased and floured 9″ round layer cake pans. Bake in moderate oven (350°) 25 to 30 minutes.

Cool layers in pan on rack 10 minutes; then remove from pans. Frost with Orange Butter Cream Frosting. Makes 12 to 16 servings.

**Orange Butter Cream Frosting:** Cream ½ c. butter. Gradually add 3 c. sifted confectioners sugar alternately with ⅓ c. orange juice concentrate, thawed, creaming well after each addition until mixture is light and fluffy.

## SAUERKRAUT SURPRISE CAKE

*The sauerkraut gives the cake a velvety crumb . . . delicious*

½ c. butter or regular
margarine
1½ c. sugar
3 eggs
1 tsp. vanilla
2 c. sifted flour
½ c. cocoa
1 tsp. baking powder

1 tsp. baking soda
¼ tsp. salt
1 c. water
1 (8 oz.) can sauerkraut,
drained, rinsed twice and
snipped fine
Chocolate Sour Cream Frosting
(recipe follows)

Cream together butter and sugar. Beat in eggs one at a time; beat well. Add vanilla.

Sift together flour, cocoa, baking powder, soda and salt. Add to creamed mixture alternately with water, beating after each addition. Stir in sauerkraut.

Grease 13×9×2″ pan. Bake in moderate oven (350°) for 35 to 40 minutes. Frost with Chocolate Sour Cream Frosting. Makes 16 servings.

**Chocolate Sour Cream Frosting:** Melt 1 (6 oz.) pkg. semisweet chocolate pieces and 4 tblsp. butter over water in a double boiler. Remove and blend in ½ c. dairy sour cream. Add 1 tsp. vanilla and ¼ tsp. salt. Gradually add enough sifted confectioners sugar (about 2½–3 c.) to make frosting of spreading consistency.

## SAUSAGE CAKE

*Aging mellows the flavor of this hearty cake that men will like*

| | |
|---|---|
| 1 lb. bulk pork sausage | 1 tsp. ground allspice |
| 1½ c. sugar | 1 tsp. ground cloves |
| 1½ c. brown sugar, firmly packed | 1 tsp. ground nutmeg |
| | 1 c. chopped pecans |
| 1 tsp. baking soda | 1 c. raisins |
| ½ c. buttermilk | ½ c. hot double-strength coffee |
| 3 c. sifted flour | Butter Glaze (recipe follows) |
| 1 tsp. ground cinnamon | |

Combine sausage with sugars; blend well.

Dissolve baking soda in buttermilk.

Sift together 2 c. flour and spices. Combine remaining 1 c. flour with nuts and raisins, coating well.

Add dry ingredients to sausage-sugar mixture alternately with buttermilk and coffee. Stir in nuts and raisins. Pour into greased 13×9×2″ pan. Bake in moderate oven (350°) 1 hour, or until cake tests done. Cool on rack, then spread with Butter Glaze. Allow cake to stand at least 12 hours before serving. Makes 16 servings.

**Butter Glaze:** Combine 2 c. sifted confectioners sugar, 1½ tsp. vanilla, 3 tblsp. milk and 3 tblsp. softened butter. Beat until smooth.

## MARBLE CAKE

*Serve with chocolate ice cream and a sprinkling of chopped pecans*

| | |
|---|---|
| 2 c. sugar | ¾ c. milk |
| 4 eggs, separated | 1 tsp. almond extract |
| ½ c. butter | Bread crumbs |
| 2 c. sifted flour | ½ c. cocoa |
| 2 tsp. baking powder | 1 tblsp. milk |
| ¼ tsp. salt | Sifted confectioners sugar |

Cream together sugar, egg yolks and butter.

Sift together flour, baking powder and salt. Add alternately with ¾ c. milk to creamed mixture, ending with flour mixture. Add almond extract.

Beat egg whites until stiff but not dry; fold into batter. Turn half of batter into well-buttered 10″ tube pan that has been sprinkled with bread crumbs all around tube part.

Combine cocoa and 1 tblsp. milk; add to remaining batter; blend well. Pour over white batter in tube pan. Bake in moderate oven (350°) 1 hour and 10 minutes, or until cake tests done. Cool in pan 10 minutes, then turn out on platter, crusty side up. Sprinkle cooled cake with confectioners sugar. Makes 10 to 12 servings.

## CARROT/PECAN CAKE

*A spiced nut cake that keeps well if you hide it—a real treat*

| | |
|---|---|
| 1¼ c. salad oil | 2 tsp. ground cinnamon |
| 2 c. sugar | 4 eggs |
| 2 c. sifted flour | 3 c. grated raw carrots |
| 2 tsp. baking powder | 1 c. finely chopped pecans |
| 1 tsp. baking soda | Orange Glaze (recipe follows) |
| 1 tsp. salt | |

Combine oil and sugar; mix well.

Sift together remaining dry ingredients. Sift half of dry ingredients into sugar mixture; blend. Sift in remaining dry ingredients alternately with eggs, one at a time, mixing well after each addition.

Add carrots and mix well; then mix in pecans. Pour into lightly oiled 10″ tube pan. Bake in slow oven (325°) about 1 hour and 10 minutes. Cool in pan upright on rack. Remove from pan.

Split cake in 3 horizontal layers. Spread Orange Glaze between layers and on top and sides. Makes 10 to 12 servings.

**Orange Glaze:** Combine 1 c. sugar and ¼ c. cornstarch in saucepan. Slowly add 1 c. orange juice and 1 tsp. lemon juice and stir until smooth. Add 2 tblsp. butter, 2 tblsp. grated orange peel and ½ tsp. salt. Cook over low heat until thick and glossy. Cool before spreading on cake.

## CHOCOLATE FUDGE TREATS

*These bars will be sold at the bazaar as fast as you can unpack them*

| | |
|---|---|
| 1 c. sifted flour | 2 squares unsweetened |
| 1 c. sugar |    chocolate, melted |
| ½ tsp. salt | ½ tsp. vanilla |
| ½ tsp. baking soda | ½ c. chopped walnuts |
| ½ c. dairy sour cream | ½ c. semisweet chocolate pieces |
| ¼ c. shortening | ½ c. flaked coconut |
| ⅓ c. water | ½ tsp. ground cinnamon |
| 2 eggs | |

Sift together flour, sugar, salt and baking soda. Add sour cream, shortening, water and eggs. Beat at medium speed for 2 minutes. Add chocolate and vanilla; beat for 2 minutes. Pour into greased and floured 13×9×2″ cake pan. Combine walnuts, chocolate bits, coconut and cinnamon. Sprinkle over cake batter.

Bake in moderate oven (350°) for 20 to 25 minutes. Cool and cut into 2×1½″ bars. Makes 30.

## PEANUT SPONGE SQUARES

*A lovely company dessert. Pretty enough for a shower or anniversary*

| | |
|---|---|
| 6 eggs, separated | 2 tsp. baking powder |
| 2 c. sugar | ¼ tsp. salt |
| 3 tblsp. lemon juice | Thin Icing (recipe follows) |
| 1 tsp. grated lemon peel | 1 (13 oz.) can salted peanuts, |
| ⅓ c. hot water |    chopped |
| 2 c. sifted flour | |

Beat egg yolks until thick and lemon-colored. Add sugar gradually and beat well. Add lemon juice and peel. Pour in water and beat well.

Sift flour, baking powder and salt together. Add to egg yolk mixture, beating at low speed. Beat egg whites until stiff but not dry. Fold into batter.

Pour into greased and floured 13×9×2″ cake pan. Bake in moderate oven (350°) for 35 to 40 minutes or until cake tests done. Cool for 10 minutes then turn out on rack to cool completely.

Cut into 48 squares and spread with Thin Icing on all sides; roll in chopped peanuts. Makes 48 squares.

**Thin Icing:** Combine 1 lb. confectioners sugar, 2 tsp. vanilla, pinch of salt and 5 to 6 tblsp. milk. Mix well to make a thin icing.

CHAPTER 7

# Cakes Your Guests Will Remember

Country women excel in creating high, light and fluffy cakes. Always on the lookout for an unusual recipe, they have the knack of turning a perfectly acceptable cake into a masterpiece. Sometimes it's just an extra pinch of spice or a second tablespoon of lemon juice or a mite more vanilla that makes the difference. We've eaten our way across country sampling cakes and have collected an outstanding number of "the best cakes I've ever eaten." Each and every one of these cake recipes will add to your reputation for being a fine cake baker.

Rocky Mountain Cake, a five-star beauty, is a marvelous blend of unique flavors—a touch of caraway seeds, spices, lots of eggs and butter. Finish it off with generous swirls of brown sugar frosting blanketed with chopped black walnuts—just plain delicious.

Three Southern specialties include updated versions of the traditional Lord and Lady Baltimore Cakes made from a mix, and a smooth velvety Fig Cake with a buttermilk base that gives it the extra velvety crumb—a tawny beauty you'll be proud to serve. Chocolate Cake Ring and Walnut Cake Ring can be teamed together to make a double-ring wedding or engagement party cake—a beautiful duo. And don't miss our special Fudge Ribbon Cake—a $1500 winner in a national baking contest. The deep dark delicious chocolate layers have a satiny cream cheese filling. Your guests will give you five stars of approval when they taste this!

For the holidays present our Italian Cream Cake—five layers tall with two fillings, chocolate spice and lemon fruit—a dream of a cake that is feather light, yet rich and creamy. You'll want to make our Grand Champion Sponge Cake again and again. Gossamer light, this handsome cake won a purple ribbon at the state fair—it was chosen finest in its class. Still another fair winner is Blue Ribbon Banana Cake, mellow flavored with a creamy nut filling, frosted with a drift of white icing. Usher in the strawberry season with Elegant Strawberry Torte—brown sugar layers crunchy with nuts, filled and topped with whipped cream and wreathed with strawberries.

In this chapter of quality cakes you'll find one for every situation, every one is a winner. And, of course, if you've just finished freezing homemade ice cream, a generous scoopful combined with a slice of cake makes a dessert that company will remember.

## CREATE A LUSCIOUS CAKE ROLL

You'll be a mighty proud to serve any one of these four beautiful cake rolls. Frozen Cake Roll, Four Ways would be great to serve at a huge buffet. Make up all the variations and freeze until the big day. With the top sparkling with Amber Candy Shatters, Coffee and Cream Ginger Roll is a lovely fall dessert. Elegant Chocolate Log and Walnut Cream Roll fit into any season or any situation.

### FROZEN CAKE ROLL, FOUR WAYS

*These spectacular cake rolls are great to keep in the freezer for unexpected dinner guests.*

| | |
|---|---|
| 4 eggs, separated | ¾ c. sifted cake flour |
| ¾ c. sugar | ¾ tsp. baking powder |
| 1 tsp. vanilla | ¼ tsp. salt |

Beat egg yolks until light and lemon-colored. Slowly add sugar, beating until creamy. Add vanilla; beat.

Sift together flour and baking powder; gradually add to sugar mixture. Beat only until smooth.

Beat egg whites with salt until stiff, but not dry. Fold into batter.

Spread batter evenly in greased 15½ × 10½ × 1″ jelly roll pan lined with heavily greased brown paper.

Bake in moderate oven (375°) 15 minutes, or until top springs back when lightly touched. Loosen cake edges at once; invert onto clean towel sprinkled with confectioners sugar. Cut off hard edges. Roll up, leaving towel in; cool. Unroll; fill with strawberry filling (see Strawberry Roll); reroll.

Wrap and freeze, seam side down. To serve, take from freezer, spread top with Strawberry Sauce, slice. Makes 1 roll, or 10 (1″) slices. Repeat recipe for Pineapple and Butterscotch Rolls.

NOTE: You can freeze unfilled cake rolls, 6 months; filled rolls, up to 1 month.

**Chocolate Cake Roll:** Follow above recipe, sifting ¼ c. cocoa with flour.

## CAKE ROLL FILLINGS, SAUCES

**Basic Filling:** Whip 1 c. heavy cream until it begins to thicken. Gradually add 3 tblsp. sugar and ¼ tsp. vanilla (use almond extract instead of vanilla for Pineapple Roll); beat stiff.

**Strawberry Roll:** Fold 1 (10 oz.) pkg. frozen strawberry slices, drained, into Basic Filling. Spread on cake; roll. Bring to boil ¼ c. strawberry jam and ¼ c. light corn syrup; brush on top of roll. Serve with Strawberry Sauce.

**Strawberry Sauce:** Mix 1 c. strawberry jam and 1 c. light corn syrup; bring to boil. Cool. Makes 1 pint.

**Pineapple Roll:** Fold 1 (8¼ oz.) can crushed pineapple, drained, into Basic Filling. Spread over cake; roll. For glaze, bring to boil ¼ c. apricot jam and ¼ c. light corn syrup; brush on top of roll. Serve with Pineapple Sauce.

**Pineapple Sauce:** Mix 1 (8¼ oz.) can crushed pineapple, drained, with 1 c. light corn syrup. Bring to boil and cook until mixture thickens. Makes 1 pint.

**Butterscotch Roll:** Fold 1 (3 oz.) can chopped pecans into Basic Filling. Spread over cake; roll. For glaze, heat ¼ c. light corn syrup and 1 tblsp. melted butter or regular margarine. Brush on top of roll. Sprinkle with ¼ c. chopped pecans. Serve with Butterscotch Sauce.

**Butterscotch Sauce:** Combine ⅔ c. light corn syrup, 1¼ c. brown sugar, firmly packed, ¼ c. butter and ¼ tsp. salt; boil to heavy syrup; cool. Add 1 (6 oz.) can evaporated milk. Makes about 1 pint.

**Chocolate Roll:** Spread Basic Filling over cake; roll. Sift ¼ c. confectioners sugar over roll. Serve with Chocolate Sauce.

**Chocolate Sauce:** Put 4 squares unsweetened chocolate, ½ c. butter and 2¼ c. evaporated milk in top of double boiler; heat until butter and chocolate melt. Slowly add 3 c. sugar; heat until sugar dissolves. Cool; refrigerate. (Sauce will thicken. If too thick, thin with corn syrup.) Makes 1 quart.

N O T E : Cake rolls may be filled with different kinds of ice cream, softened just enough to spread, and returned to the freezer. Serve sliced with a sundae sauce.

## COFFEE AND CREAM GINGER ROLL

*Old-fashioned gingerbread rolled around a whipped cream filling*

| | |
|---|---|
| 5 eggs, separated | 1 tsp. ground nutmeg |
| ½ tsp. cream of tartar | 1 tsp. ground cardamom |
| 1 c. sifted confectioners sugar | (optional) |
| 3 tblsp. sifted flour | ½ tsp. ground cloves |
| ¼ tsp. salt | Sifted confectioners sugar |
| $\frac{1}{16}$ tsp. ground black pepper | 1½ c. heavy cream |
| 1½ tblsp. instant coffee | ½ c. sifted confectioners sugar |
| 1½ tsp. ground ginger | 1½ tsp. vanilla |
| 1 tsp. ground allspice | Amber Candy Shatters (recipe |
| 1 tsp. ground cinnamon | follows) |

Beat egg whites (at room temperature) with cream of tartar until soft peaks form. Gradually add ½ c. sifted confectioners sugar, beating until stiff peaks form.

In a separate bowl, beat egg yolks until thick and light colored.

Sift together 3 times the remaining ½ c. confectioners sugar, flour, salt, pepper, coffee and spices. Fold into egg yolks until just blended. Gently fold yolk mixture into egg whites. Spread gently and evenly in a 15½ ×10½ ×1″ jelly roll pan which has been greased, lined with waxed paper and the waxed paper greased.

Bake in moderate oven (350°) 15 minutes or until cake springs back when touched lightly. Turn out on a towel sprinkled with sifted confectioners sugar. Quickly and gently peel off paper. Starting at narrow end, roll cake and towel together; cool thoroughly on rack.

Whip heavy cream, gradually adding the ½ c. confectioners sugar and vanilla. Unroll cake and spread with cream. Roll up again and roll onto serving platter. Chill thoroughly, at least 3 hours.

Sprinkle lightly with confectioners sugar. Slice to serve and top with Amber Candy Shatters, or accompany each slice with fruits. Makes 10 servings.

**Amber Candy Shatters:** In a heavy frypan, cook ½ c. sugar over medium heat, stirring, until sugar melts and turns a golden brown (be careful not to scorch). Pour into buttered shallow pan to cool and harden. Break into pieces, then crush with rolling pin.

## ELEGANT CHOCOLATE LOG

*Share the beauty of this chocolate roll with very special guests*

| | |
|---|---|
| 1¼ c. sifted confectioners sugar | 1 c. heavy cream, whipped |
| ¼ c. plus 1 tblsp. sifted flour | 2 tblsp. sugar (about) |
| ½ tsp. salt | 8 to 12 marshmallows, cut up |
| 5 tblsp. cocoa | 1 square unsweetened chocolate |
| 6 eggs, separated | 2 c. confectioners sugar |
| ¼ tsp. cream of tartar | Light cream |
| 1¼ tsp. vanilla | ¼ c. finely chopped pecans |
| 1 tblsp. water | |

Sift 1¼ c. confectioners sugar, flour, salt and cocoa together 3 times.

Beat egg whites with cream of tartar until stiff.

Beat egg yolks until thick and lemon-colored; beat in vanilla and water. Add sifted dry ingredients and beat into egg yolks until well blended. Fold in beaten egg whites.

Pour into greased and paper-lined 15½ × 10½ × 1" jelly roll pan. Bake in moderate oven (375°) 15 to 20 minutes. Lightly dust clean dish towel with confectioners sugar; loosen cake around edges with spatula. Invert on towel. Lift off pan and carefully peel off paper. With a sharp knife, cut off cake's crisp edges. Roll up cake gently, from narrow end, by folding edge of cake over and then tucking it in; continue rolling cake, lifting towel higher with one hand as you guide the rolling with the other hand, rolling the towel in the cake (to prevent cake sticking). Let cool on rack (wrap tightly in towel to hold it in shape).

Unroll cake on towel; spread with whipped cream, sweetened to taste with 2 tblsp. sugar and with marshmallows added. Roll like jelly roll.

For frosting, melt chocolate; add 2 c. confectioners sugar with enough light cream to make it spreadable. Spread over cake and immediately sprinkle with chopped nuts. Makes 8 to 10 servings.

## WALNUT CREAM ROLL

*Wonderful to serve during the holidays—also makes a special gift*

| | |
|---|---|
| ¼ tsp. salt | ½ tsp. vanilla |
| 4 eggs, separated | 2 tblsp. sugar |
| ⅔ c. confectioners sugar | Cream Filling (recipe follows) |
| 2 tblsp. flour | Walnut halves |
| 1 c. walnuts, chopped medium fine | |

Add salt to egg whites; beat at high speed until stiff; beat in 2 tblsp. confectioners sugar.

Beat yolks until thick and light, then beat in rest of confectioners sugar; fold into egg white mixture. Sprinkle flour and walnuts over surface, then fold in; add vanilla.

Grease 15½×10½×1″ jelly roll pan; line with waxed paper; grease paper and sprinkle with 2 tblsp. sugar. Spread batter evenly in pan.

Bake in moderate oven (350°) 20 minutes. Turn out at once onto damp, clean towel heavily coated with confectioners sugar; roll cake up gently inside towel; cool. Unroll to fill.

Spread ¾ of Cream Filling over cake surface; reroll. Spread remaining filling over outside. Decorate with walnut halves, candied cherries or slivers of citron. Makes 8 servings.

**Cream Filling:** Blend 1½ c. heavy cream, whipped, ¼ c. sugar and ½ tsp. vanilla. Or, if you prefer, use peppermint extract instead of vanilla, and tint with a few drops of green food color.

NOTE: You can freeze the filled and frosted cake for a few days. Freeze it unwrapped and then package it carefully, seal and re-freeze.

## TORTES AND MORE TORTES

A handsome collection of whipped cream-decked desserts—every one as pretty as a picture. Plan to fix the Orange Angel Torte for an occasion when twenty-four guests are coming for dessert.

### ORANGE ANGEL TORTE

*Fix the base for this lovely torte one day and the filling the next*

1 c. thinly sliced candied red
   and green cherries
1½ c. chopped nuts
2 c. flaked coconut
¾ c. fine soft white bread
   crumbs
6 egg whites
1 tsp. cream of tartar
½ tsp. salt

2 c. sugar
1 tsp. vinegar
1 tsp. vanilla
Orange Filling (recipe follows)
2 c. heavy cream, whipped, or
   2 envelopes dessert topping
   mix, whipped
Cherry Flowers (recipe follows)

Line a 15½ × 10½ × 1″ jelly roll pan with brown paper; grease and lightly flour paper.

Combine fruit, nuts, coconut and crumbs in a large bowl; mix to coat fruit, nuts and coconut with crumbs.

Bring egg whites to room temperature. Add cream of tartar and salt. Beat at high speed of electric mixer or portable beater to soft peak stage. Slowly beat in sugar, vinegar and vanilla. Beat 10 minutes to the stiff peak stage. Fold into the fruit-nut mixture.

Turn mixture into the prepared pan. Spread evenly over paper, building the edges higher. Bake in moderate oven (375°) 25 minutes, or until lightly browned. Cool. Transfer torte to a tray; cut paper from edges, but not from bottom.

Spread chilled Orange Filling over the top to the raised edges. Cover with whipped cream or dessert topping mix, prepared by package directions. Decorate with Cherry Flowers. Refrigerate overnight before serving, or freeze unwrapped, then wrap for storage. Thaw 30 minutes before serving frozen torte. Makes 24 servings.

**Orange Filling:** Mix ½ c. flour, 1½ c. sugar and ½ tsp. salt in saucepan. Gradually add 2½ c. orange juice, then 6 slightly beaten egg yolks (½ c.) and 2 tblsp. butter or margarine. Cook over medium heat until thick. Cover and cool, then refrigerate.

**Cherry Flowers:** Cut 12 red candied cherries in quarters, 3 green candied cherries in eighths. Group 2 red slices and 1 green slice together on top of Orange Angel Torte to make 24 flowers, one for each serving.

## ELEGANT STRAWBERRY TORTE

*A brown sugar cake dressed up with whipped cream and berries*

| | |
|---|---|
| 3 c. sifted cake flour | 1 tsp. baking soda |
| 2 c. brown sugar, firmly packed | ½ c. chopped nuts |
| ½ tsp. salt | 2 c. heavy cream, whipped and |
| 1 c. butter | sweetened |
| 1 egg, slightly beaten | 1 pt. fresh strawberries, sliced |
| 1 c. sour milk | |

Mix together flour, brown sugar, salt and butter. Set aside 1 c. crumb mixture.

Combine egg, milk and baking soda. Add to crumb mixture; stir well. Pour into 2 greased and paper-lined 9″ round layer cake pans. Sprinkle with reserved crumb mixture; then nuts. Bake in moderate oven (375°) 25 to 30 minutes, or until cake tests done. Cool.

Place one layer, nut side up on serving plate. Spread with half of the whipped cream. Top with sliced strawberries. Place other layer on top. Spoon remaining whipped cream into puffs around cake. Garnish with sliced strawberries. Serve immediately. Makes 12 servings.

## CHOCOLATE/CHERRY TORTE

*This special-occasion beauty will serve 12. Keep in refrigerator*

| | |
|---|---|
| 1 tblsp. flour | 1½ c. sugar |
| ½ tblsp. cocoa | 2 eggs |
| 2 c. sifted cake flour | 4 squares unsweetened |
| ¾ tsp. salt | chocolate, melted |
| 2 tsp. baking powder | 1⅓ c. evaporated milk |
| 1 (4 oz.) bottle maraschino | 2 tsp. red food color |
| cherries | Devil's Creme (recipe follows) |
| ½ c. butter | |

Combine 1 tblsp. flour and cocoa. Lightly grease two 9" round layer cake pans; dust with flour-cocoa mixture.

Sift together 2 c. cake flour, salt and baking powder. Set aside.

Drain cherries, reserving juice. Chop cherries and set aside.

Cream butter; gradually add sugar and blend until light and fluffy. Add eggs, chocolate, evaporated milk, reserved cherry juice and food color. Beat until smooth. Blend in dry ingredients. Fold in cherries.

Bake in prepared pans in moderate oven (350°) for 25 to 30 minutes. Remove from pans and cool on racks. Carefully split cake layers.

Put layers together and top with Devil's Creme; reserve ½ c. to decorate top. We used a cake decorator—✳30 tip—to pipe frosting on. Decorate with chocolate candy kisses. Refrigerate to set Creme. Makes 12 servings.

**Devil's Creme:** Stir together ¼ c. powdered chocolate drink mix, ¼ c. sifted confectioners sugar, 1 tsp. vanilla and 2 c. heavy cream. Chill; whip until stiff.

### GINGERBREAD TORTE

*Gingerbread layers separated with orange-flavored chocolate icing*

1 (14 oz.) pkg. gingerbread mix    2 tblsp. melted butter
1 tsp. ground ginger    Orange-Sliver Chocolate Icing
1 tsp. ground cinnamon    (recipe follows)

Stir together gingerbread mix, ginger and cinnamon. Then prepare gingerbread according to package directions, except add the 2 tblsp. melted butter along with the water called for in package directions.

Pour into greased 9" round layer cake pan. Bake according to package directions.

Cool in pan for 10 minutes, then remove from pan and cool on rack. When cake is cool, place on serving platter; spoon Orange-Sliver Chocolate Icing over top, allowing it to drizzle down cake sides. Makes 8 servings.

**Orange-Sliver Chocolate Icing:** Combine ½ c. orange marmalade, ½ c. semisweet chocolate pieces and a few grains of salt in top of double boiler. Heat over hot water, stirring occasionally until chocolate melts and mixture is shiny.

## ORANGE/BUTTERSCOTCH TORTE

*Make this lucious dessert a day ahead—it serves at least 18*

6 eggs
1¼ c. sugar
¾ tsp. almond extract
¼ c. sifted flour
1 tsp. baking powder
¼ tsp. salt

2 c. graham cracker crumbs
1 c. chopped walnuts
Orange-Butterscotch Sauce
   (recipe follows)
2 c. heavy cream

Beat eggs on high speed of electric mixer for 5 minutes. Gradually add sugar, beating until soft peaks form (about 5 minutes). Add almond extract.

Sift together flour, baking powder and salt; add graham cracker crumbs. Fold crumb mixture, about ½ c. at a time, into beaten eggs. Fold in nuts. Pour into greased 13×9×2" baking pan.

Bake in slow oven (325°) 30 to 35 minutes. Cool; turn out on plate.

Make Orange/Butterscotch Sauce. Spread two thirds of sauce over cake.

Whip heavy cream until stiff peaks form. Spread whipped cream over top and sides of cake. Dribble remaining sauce in lines over whipped cream; cut through whipped cream with knife several times for a marbleized effect.

Refrigerate at least 8 hours. Cut into 18 to 21 pieces.

**Orange/Butterscotch Sauce:** Combine in saucepan 1 c. brown sugar, firmly packed, ¼ c. butter, ½ c. frozen orange juice concentrate, 2 tblsp. flour, 1 beaten egg and ¼ tsp. salt. Bring to boil over medium heat; cook until thick (about 4 minutes), stirring constantly. Cool slightly.

## FRUIT/NUT TORTE

*Nut curls for garnish: Shave nuts thin with vegetable parer*

1 c. Brazil nuts, halved, or ¾ c. whole blanched almonds

2 c. walnut or pecan halves

1 c. whole candied red and green cherries, mixed

1 c. raisins or sliced dates

1½ c. sifted flour

1 tsp. salt

4 eggs

2 egg yolks

1¼ c. sugar

1 tblsp. vanilla

2 egg whites

¼ c. sugar

¼ c. sifted confectioners sugar

1 tblsp. sugar (for top)

¼ c. Brazil nuts curls (for top)

Fit two lengths of brown paper into a 9" square pan; allow 1½" extension beyond pan edges. Grease lightly to settle papers into the pan.

Combine nuts and fruit in a large bowl. Toss with ½ c. flour. Sift remaining 1 c. flour with the salt.

Beat eggs and egg yolks until thick and lemon-colored. Gradually beat in 1¼ c. sugar and vanilla, beating until cream-colored. Fold in dry ingredients. Pour over the fruit-nut mixture; fold until completely mixed. Turn into prepared pan.

Bake in moderate oven (375°) 50 to 60 minutes, or until cake tester comes out clean when inserted in center of the torte. (When the torte is a medium brown, cover it with paper or foil for remainder of baking time.)

Meanwhile, prepare topping. Beat egg whites until peaks form. Gradually beat in ¼ c. sugar and the confectioners sugar; continue beating until stiff and glossy.

Take torte from the oven, remove paper cover and spread the topping evenly over crust. Be sure to cover edges. Sprinkle with remaining 1 tblsp. sugar and Brazil nut curls. Return to oven for 15 minutes, or until lightly browned.

Cool in pan 30 minutes. Lift from pan by paper liner onto wire rack. Loosen paper from meringue edges. When cold, cut paper off sides, but leave it on the bottom of the torte. Serve cut in slices or small squares, plain or topped with whipped cream. Makes 24 servings.

## CHOCOLATE CREAM TORTE

*This chocolate fantasy will add a note of beauty to your buffet*

| | |
|---|---|
| 1 c. shortening | 2 tsp. warm water |
| 3 c. sugar | 10 egg whites |
| 4 c. sifted flour | 1 tsp. vanilla |
| 1½ tsp. cream of tartar | Chocolate Cream Filling (recipe |
| 1 c. buttermilk | follows) |
| 1½ tsp. baking soda | |

Cream together shortening and sugar until light and fluffy.

Sift together flour and cream of tartar 3 times. Add to creamed mixture alternately with buttermilk.

Dissolve baking soda in warm water. Add to batter. Beat egg whites until stiff. Fold into batter; add vanilla.

Pour into four 9″ round layer cake pans. Bake in moderate oven (350°) for 30 to 35 minutes or until cakes test done. Cool. Spread layers with Chocolate Cream Filling. If you wish, frost sides with your favorite 7-minute frosting. Makes 12 servings.

### Chocolate Cream Filling

| | |
|---|---|
| 1 c. sugar | 1½ tblsp. butter |
| 2 egg yolks, beaten | 1 c. light cream |
| 2 squares unsweetened | 1 tsp. vanilla |
| chocolate | |

Combine first 5 ingredients. Cook over low heat, stirring constantly. When thickened, remove from heat. Add vanilla. Beat well.

# FEATHER-LIGHT ANGELS

Three gorgeous angel food cakes that stand tall and handsome. Each would make a beautiful birthday cake. Let each family member choose his favorite for his big day.

## PEPPERMINT ANGEL FOOD CAKE

*This delicate pink and white beauty is a must for bridal showers*

| | |
|---|---|
| 1 c. sifted cake flour | 1 tsp. vanilla |
| 1 c. sifted confectioners sugar | ½ tsp. peppermint extract |
| 1⅔ c. egg whites (about 12) | 12 drops red food color |
| 1½ tsp. cream of tartar | Two-Toned Swirl Frosting |
| ¼ tsp. salt | (recipe follows) |
| 1 c. sugar | |

Sift together cake flour and confectioners sugar 4 times.

Combine egg whites, cream of tartar and salt in a large mixing bowl. Beat until egg whites are stiff but not dry. Beat in sugar, 2 tblsp. at a time, mixing well after each addition. Add flour mixture in 4 parts, folding about 15 strokes with each addition.

Divide batter in half. Fold vanilla into one half. Fold peppermint extract and red food color in other half. Drop batter by alternate spoonfuls in an ungreased 10″ tube pan. Pull metal spatula through batter, swirling gently. Bake in slow oven (325°) for 50 minutes, or until cake tests done. Invert on rack to cool. Frost with Two-Toned Swirl Frosting. Makes 10 to 12 servings.

**Two-Toned Swirl Frosting:** Prepare your favorite 7-minute frosting or fluffy white frosting mix, adding 2 drops peppermint extract. Tint frosting pale pink with red food color. Remove ½ c. frosting and tint dark pink. Frost cake with pale pink frosting. Using a spoon, swirl dark pink frosting over cake.

## PARTY ANGEL FOOD CAKE

*A lovely angel food studded with bits of cherries and pecans*

| | |
|---|---|
| 1 c. plus 2 tblsp. sifted cake flour | 1 c. sugar |
| ¾ c. sugar | 1 tsp. vanilla |
| 1⅔ c. egg whites (about 12) | ½ tsp. almond extract |
| 1½ tsp. cream of tartar | 10 maraschino cherries, cut up |
| ½ tsp. salt | ½ c. chopped pecans |
| | Maraschino cherries with stems |

Sift together cake flour and ¾ c. sugar 4 times.

Combine egg whites, cream of tartar and salt in a large mixing bowl. Beat until egg whites are stiff but not dry. Add 1 c. sugar,

2 tblsp. at a time, mixing well after each addition. Mix in vanilla and almond extract. Add flour mixture in 4 parts, folding about 15 strokes with each addition.

Fold in cut-up cherries and pecans. Turn into an ungreased 10" tube pan and pull metal spatula through batter once to break air bubbles. Bake in moderate oven (350°) 45 minutes or until cake tests done. Cool inverted. Frost with your favorite fluffy white frosting; garnish with maraschino cherries. Makes 10 to 12 servings.

## ORANGE DREAM ANGEL FOOD CAKE

*A hint of orange makes this lovely marbled cake very popular*

| | |
|---|---|
| 1¼ c. egg whites (about 10) | 1½ tblsp. grated orange peel |
| ½ tsp. salt | ½ tsp. almond extract |
| 1¼ tsp. cream of tartar | Yellow food color |
| 1 c. sugar | Red food color |
| 1 c. sifted cake flour | Orange Fluffy Frosting (recipe |
| ½ c. sugar | follows) |
| 1 tsp. vanilla | |

Beat egg whites with salt and cream of tartar until stiff but not dry. Gradually add 1 c. sugar, beating well after each addition.

Sift together flour and ½ c. sugar 3 times; fold into egg whites. Divide batter in half. Add vanilla to one half.

Add orange peel and almond extract to other half. Combine yellow and red food colors to make orange, and stir into batter.

Alternate orange and white batter in an ungreased 10" tube pan. Bake in moderate oven (350°) 45 minutes, or until a finger pressed lightly on top leaves no impression.

Invert on rack and cool before removing from pan. Frost with Orange Fluffy Frosting. Makes 10 to 12 servings.

**Orange Fluffy Frosting:** Beat 1 (3 oz.) pkg. cream cheese until light and fluffy. Gradually add 1½ c. sifted confectioners sugar; beat well. Stir in 1 tblsp. grated orange peel. If too thick, add a few drops orange juice to make frosting of spreading consistency.

# FESTIVE HOLIDAY CAKES

'Tis the season to make your treasured cakes to grace the holiday table. We offer a grand assortment of fruitcakes, one a no-bake and another baked in individual cans—all are just perfect to give to a friend or neighbor for a homemade treat.

## FROZEN FRUITCAKE

*Busy women delight in this quick, no-bake cake—a holiday favorite*

| | |
|---|---|
| 2 c. milk | 2 c. vanilla wafer or macaroon |
| ½ c. sugar | crumbs |
| ¼ c. flour | ½ c. candied red cherries, |
| ¼ tsp. salt | halved |
| 2 eggs, beaten | ¼ c. candied mixed fruits |
| 1 tsp. vanilla | 1 c. broken pecans |
| 1 c. light raisins | 1 c. heavy cream, whipped |

Scald milk in top of double boiler.

Mix together sugar, flour and salt; add to milk all at once. Cook over hot water about 3 minutes until smooth and medium thick, stirring constantly.

Pour hot mixture over beaten eggs and return to double boiler. Cook until thick, about 3 minutes, stirring constantly. Add vanilla. Cool.

Stir raisins, crumbs, cherries, mixed fruits and nuts into cooked mixture.

Fold in cream. Pour into greased and waxed paper-lined 8½ × 4½×2½″ loaf pan. Cool completely; and freeze. Makes 8 servings.

NOTE: To decorate top of fruit cake, arrange a few whole nut meats and candied red and green cherries on waxed paper in bottom of mold before pouring in batter.

## GOLDEN MINIATURES

*You can bake these little cakes in soup cans at the last minute*

| | |
|---|---|
| 4 c. sifted flour | 12 eggs |
| 2 tsp. baking powder | 1 tblsp. grated lemon peel |
| 1½ tsp. ground nutmeg | 3 c. coarsely chopped pecans |
| 2 tsp. ground cinnamon | Candied Pineapple, cut up |
| ½ tsp. salt | (recipe follows) |
| 2 c. butter | Candied Cherries, halved (recipe |
| 2 c. brown sugar, firmly packed | follows) |

Sift together flour, baking powder, nutmeg, cinnamon and salt. Reserve ⅓ c. of this mixture.

Cream butter and brown sugar. Add eggs, one at a time, beating well. Gradually add flour mixture, mixing well. Add lemon peel.

Toss ⅓ c. flour with fruit-nut mixture. Stir into batter.

Spoon into 12 greased and floured 10½-oz. cans, filling 1″ from top. Bake in very slow oven (275°) 1 hour 15 minutes, or until cakes test done. Cool on racks. Decorate with Candied Pineapple and Cherries.

NOTE: Before serving, you can frost fruit cakes with an icing made by combining 2 c. sifted confectioners sugar, 1 tblsp. soft butter, 1 tblsp. milk and ½ tsp. vanilla. Blend well. Drizzle over cakes. Decorate with candied fruit. Makes 12.

**Candied Pineapple and Cherries:** Drain 2 (1 lb. 14 oz.) cans sliced pineapple; reserve syrup. Combine 2 c. sugar, ½ c. light corn syrup and 1⅔ c. pineapple syrup in a heavy 10″ skillet. Cook over medium heat, stirring constantly, until mixture boils. Cook until temperature reaches 234° on candy thermometer. Add a third of the pineapple slices; bring to a boil. Reduce heat; simmer 25 minutes or until pineapple is transparent around edges. Remove from skillet; drain on wire rack. Repeat with remaining pineapple, cooking a third at a time. Then add 3 (8 oz.) jars maraschino cherries, drained. Simmer for 25 minutes. Let dry 24 hours at room temperature.

## ENGLISH CURRANT CAKE

*Serve this fruit-flavored cake to guests at your next tea party*

| | |
|---|---|
| 1¼ c. dried currants | 2 tsp. baking powder |
| Boiling water | ¾ tsp. salt |
| 1 c. butter or regular | 1 c. milk |
| margarine | 1½ tsp. vanilla |
| 1¾ c. sugar | 1 tblsp. grated orange peel |
| 4 eggs | 1½ tsp. grated lemon peel |
| 3½ c. sifted flour | |

Cover currants with boiling water; let stand 10 minutes.

Cream butter and sugar until light and fluffy. Add eggs, one at a time, beating well after each addition.

Sift together flour, baking powder and salt; add to creamed mixture alternately with milk and vanilla, beating 2 minutes after each addition. Stir in well-drained currants and orange and lemon peel.

Pour batter into 2 greased 9×5×3" loaf pans. Bake in moderate oven (350°) about 1 hour and 10 minutes, or until cake tests done. Cool in pans 10 minutes, then remove cakes to racks and complete cooling. Makes 12 to 16 servings.

## HOLIDAY CRANBERRY CAKE

*If you use frozen cranberries, grind them without thawing*

| | |
|---|---|
| 1 (18½ oz.) pkg. lemon cake mix | 4 eggs |
| 1 (3 oz.) pkg. cream cheese, softened | 1¼ c. ground cranberries |
| ¾ c. milk | ½ c. ground walnuts |
| | ¼ c. sugar |
| | 1 tsp. ground mace (optional) |

Blend cake mix, cream cheese and milk; beat with mixer 2 minutes at medium speed. Add eggs; blend and beat for 2 additional minutes.

Thoroughly combine cranberries, walnuts, sugar and mace; fold into cake batter. Pour into a well-greased and floured 10" tube or bundt pan. Bake in moderate oven (350°) 1 hour, or until done. Cool 5 minutes. Remove from pan. Cool on rack. Dust with confectioners sugar if you wish. Makes 10 to 12 servings.

## ORANGE CANDY CAKE

*The moist, sweet cake has a fruitcake flavor but is less expensive*

| | |
|---|---|
| 1 c. butter | 2 c. pecans, chopped |
| 2 c. sugar | 1 (4 oz.) can shredded coconut |
| 5 eggs | 4 c. sifted flour |
| 1 tblsp. vanilla | ½ tsp. baking soda |
| 1 (8 oz.) pkg. dates, cut up | 1 tsp. salt |
| 1 (1 lb.) pkg. candy orange slices, cut up | ¾ c. buttermilk |
| | Lemon Syrup (recipe follows) |

Cream butter and sugar until light and fluffy. Beat in eggs, one at a time. Add vanilla.

Mix dates, candy, nuts and coconut with ¼ c. flour.

Sift remaining flour with baking soda and salt; fold into creamed mixture alternately with buttermilk.

Fold in the date mixture. Spoon into a well-greased and floured 10″ tube pan.

Bake in slow oven (300°) 2½ hours.

Remove cake from oven and at once pour on the Lemon Syrup. Set pan on wire rack and let cool. When the cake is cooled thoroughly, remove it from the pan. Wrap snugly in aluminum foil and refrigerate 1 day or longer before serving. The flavors blend during the refrigeration and the cake slices more easily. Makes 10 to 12 servings.

**Lemon Syrup:** Mix together 1 tsp. grated lemon peel, 1 tsp. grated orange peel, ¼ c. lemon juice, ¼ c. orange juice and ½ c. confectioners sugar, sifted.

### FRUITED HONEY CAKE

*Make this moist fruitcake before the busy holidays and freeze*

| | |
|---|---|
| 3 c. seedless raisins | ½ tsp. ground mace |
| 3 c. dried currants | ½ tsp. ground allspice |
| 1¼ c. candied red cherries, quartered (½ lb.) | 1 c. shortening |
| | 1 c. honey |
| 1 c. chopped pecans or walnuts | ¼ c. brown sugar, firmly packed |
| 3 c. sifted flour | 6 eggs, beaten |
| 1½ tsp. salt | ½ c. fruit juice or canned fruit |
| 1½ tsp. baking soda | syrup |
| ½ tsp. ground cinnamon | 6 tblsp. vinegar |
| ½ tsp. ground nutmeg | |

Soften raisins and currants in boiling water; dry and cool on paper towels. Mix with cherries, nuts and ½ c. flour.

Sift together 2½ c. flour, salt, soda and spices.

Cream shortening with honey and brown sugar until fluffy. Beat in eggs.

Combine fruit juice and vinegar; add alternately with dry ingredients to creamed mixture, stirring well after each addition. Blend in fruit-nut mixture.

Pour into greased 15½×14½×4½″ pan lined with greased heavy brown paper. Bake in slow oven (300°) about 3 hours. Remove from pan; cool on rack. Freeze if desired. Makes 1 (5 lb.) cake.

## HOLIDAY FRUITCAKE

*Bake it before you get Christmas-busy—wrap and put in the freezer*

| | |
|---|---|
| 1 lb. mixed candied fruit (2 c.) | 1 tsp. ground cinnamon |
| 1 (4 oz.) can chopped citron | 1 tsp. ground cloves |
| 1 lb. dates, pitted | ½ tsp. ground nutmeg |
| ½ lb. whole candied cherries | 1 c. butter |
|   (1 c.) | 2 c. sugar |
| 1 c. raisins | 4 eggs |
| 1 c. pecan halves | 1 tsp. baking soda |
| 1 c. walnut halves | 1½ c. buttermilk |
| 4 c. sifted flour | Orange juice or apple cider |
| 1 tsp. salt | |

Prepare baking pans—you can use a 10″ tube pan or three 8×4¼×2¼″ foil pans: Cut parchment or brown paper liners for bottoms of pans; grease each paper with unsalted fat. Top with one layer waxed paper. Grease all paper and inside of pan generously.

Prepare and measure fruit; cut it in pieces the size of dates. (Leave nuts, cherries and dates whole.)

Sift together flour, salt and spices. Use enough of this flour mixture to coat all fruit pieces.

Cream butter and sugar until light and fluffy; beat in eggs, one at a time.

Add soda to remaining flour mixture; add alternately with buttermilk to creamed mixture. Mix batter with fruits and nuts. Spoon into prepared pan or pans.

To decorate, lay nuts and large fruit pieces on top of batter to form design.

Bake cake in slow oven (300°). This amount in 10″ tube pan bakes in 2½ hours, 1-lb. amounts bake in about 1¼ hours.

Cool cake out of pan on rack. When completely cool, apply orange juice or cider to entire cake with pastry brush. Wrap in waxed paper, then in foil; store in covered container in cool place. After two weeks, unwrap and baste again with orange juice or cider. Makes 12 to 16 servings.

## Variation

**Fruitcake Bonbons:** Line tiny (1¼") muffin-pan cups with paper bonbon cups. Fill three fourths full with batter. Bake in slow oven (300°) 40 to 50 minutes (place pan of water in oven so cakes stay moist). Remove from pans. Cool on rack. Remove paper cups from cakes. Set cakes on rack over foil or waxed paper. Spoon Tinted Bonbon Glaze over tops and down sides of cakes. Let stand until glaze is firm. If first coat of glaze is too thin, repeat. Glaze that drips off may be scraped up, melted over hot water and reused. Makes 11 dozen.

**Tinted Bonbon Glaze:** Mix ¼ c. water, 1 tblsp. light corn syrup, 3 c. sifted confectioners sugar and ⅛ tsp. salt in top of double boiler. Heat just until lukewarm, stirring occasionally. Remove from hot water and add 1 tsp. vanilla. Divide and tint different colors with food color. Cool slightly.


## FRUITCAKE

*Apple cider gives this fruit and nut-filled cake its superb flavor*

| | |
|---|---|
| ½ lb. candied cherries | 4 eggs |
| ½ lb. candied pineapple | 2½ c. sifted flour |
| 2¼ c. white raisins | 1 tsp. baking powder |
| 1 c. chopped walnuts | 1 tsp. ground cinnamon |
| 1 c. chopped pecans | ½ tsp. ground nutmeg |
| ½ c. sifted flour | ½ tsp. ground cloves |
| 1 c. butter or regular | ½ tsp. ground allspice |
| margarine | 1 tsp. salt |
| 2 c. light brown sugar, firmly | ¾ c. apple cider |
| packed | |

Cut all fruit and nuts in small pieces and mix with ½ c. flour, coating well.

Cream together butter and brown sugar. Add eggs, one at a time, beating well after each addition.

Sift together 2½ c. flour, baking powder, spices and salt. Add to creamed mixture alternately with apple cider. Mix well. Stir in fruit and nuts.

Pour into greased and waxed paper-lined 10″ tube pan. Bake in slow oven (275°) 3 hours. Place a small pan of water in oven under cake while it is baking. Cool on rack. Makes 12 servings.

## GRANDMOTHER'S DE LUXE CAKE

*Moist and delicious recipe passed down through the generations*

| | |
|---|---|
| 1 c. butter | ¾ tsp. salt |
| 2 c. sugar | 1 c. milk |
| 1 tsp. vanilla | 8 egg whites |
| 3¼ c. sifted flour | Tutti-Frutti Filling (recipe |
| 3½ tsp. baking powder | follows) |

Cream together butter and sugar until light and fluffy. Add vanilla. Sift together flour, baking powder and salt. Add to creamed mixture alternately with milk, beating until smooth.

Beat egg whites until stiff but not dry and fold into batter. Pour batter into 4 greased and paper-lined 9″ round cake layer pans.

Bake in moderate oven (375°) for 25 minutes or until cake tests done. Let stand 5 minutes and then turn out on racks to cool. Spread Tutti-Frutti Filling between layers and on top of cake.

**To store:** Cover loosely with foil and place in a cool place. Cake will keep several weeks and may also be frozen. Makes 12 servings.

### Tutti-Frutti Filling

| | |
|---|---|
| 8 egg yolks | 1 c. raisins |
| 1½ c. sugar | 1 c. shredded coconut |
| ½ c. butter | ½ c. chopped candied cherries |
| 1 c. chopped pecans | ¼ tsp. salt |

Beat egg yolks well. Add sugar and butter. Cook, stirring constantly, about 5 minutes until thick and clear. Remove from heat and add remaining ingredients. Cool.

## EVERYBODY'S FAVORITE FLAVORS

A rainbow of colors and flavors representing farm families' favorite cakes for special occasions. Many have been tagged with a blue ribbon, others have gained fame at church suppers and all are tender-crumbed and delicious.

### AMBROSIA-CAKE DESSERT

*Bake the cake a day ahead—so that it will be easier to split layers*

1 (9 to 12 oz.) pkg. white or yellow cake mix

1 (3¼ oz.) pkg. coconut cream pudding and pie filling

1 (3 oz.) pkg. orange flavor gelatin

1 c. hot water

¾ c. cold water

3 large bananas

Prepare cake mix as directed on package. Bake in an 8" or 9" square pan. Chill or let stand several hours so tender cake may be easily handled.

Prepare pudding as directed on package; cool.

Dissolve gelatin in hot water in bowl; add cold water. Place bowl in iced water to chill.

To assemble, split cake in half to make 2 layers (use sharp knife or a thread). Place bottom half of cake in pan in which it was baked; spread half the pudding over it. Place second layer on top; spread with remaining pudding.

Arrange layer of sliced bananas over pudding top. Spoon gelatin over bananas as soon as it reaches thick, syrupy stage. Chill until gelatin is firm.

To serve, cut in squares. Makes 9 servings.

### ITALIAN CREAM CAKE

*Here's the fancy but easy cake to make mother on her birthday*

1 (1 lb. 3 oz.) pkg. lemon chiffon cake mix

Chocolate/Spice Filling (recipe follows)

Lemon/Fruit Filling (recipe follows)

1½ c. heavy cream

¼ c. sifted confectioners sugar

Prepare cake mix according to package directions. Bake in 10″ tube pan.

When cake has cooled, remove from pan and slice in 5 layers. Fill layers alternately with Chocolate/Spice and Lemon/Fruit Filling.

Whip heavy cream with confectioners sugar; frost top and sides of cake. Chill several hours. Makes 12 to 16 servings.

**Chocolate/Spice Filling:** Prepare 1 (4 oz.) pkg. chocolate pudding and pie filling mix as directed on package, using 1½ c. milk and adding ½ tsp. ground cinnamon. Cover and cool to room temperature. Whip ½ c. heavy cream; fold into pudding. Add 2 tblsp. slivered toasted almonds. Chill 15 minutes.

**Lemon/Fruit Filling:** Prepare 1 (3¼ oz.) pkg. vanilla pudding and pie filling mix as directed on package, using 1½ c. milk. Cover and cool to room temperature. Add 2 tsp. lemon juice and 1 tblsp. grated lemon peel. Whip ½ c. heavy cream; fold into pudding. Add ⅓ c. drained pineapple tidbits and ¼ c. drained, quartered maraschino cherries. Chill 15 minutes.

## PISTACHIO CREAM CAKE

*Impress your company with this elegant layered dessert*

| | |
|---|---|
| 9 eggs, separated | ½ tsp. salt |
| 1 c. plus 2 tblsp. sugar | 1 tsp. cream of tartar |
| ¼ c. orange juice | Whipped Cream Frosting (recipe |
| Grated peel of 1 orange | follows) |
| 1 c. plus 2 tblsp. sifted flour | Unsalted pistachio nuts, chopped |

Beat egg yolks well. Add all but ⅔ c. sugar slowly, beating to mix well.

Add orange juice, peel, flour and remaining sugar. Mix well.

Add salt and cream of tartar to egg whites; beat until stiff. Fold into batter. Pour into 10″ tube pan. Bake in slow oven (300°) 1 hour. Cool on rack. Cut cooled cake in 3 layers. Spread Whipped Cream Frosting between layers, over top and sides of cake. Sprinkle nuts over top. Makes 10 to 12 servings.

**Whipped Cream Frosting:** Combine 1 c. sugar, juice and grated peel of 1 orange, ¼ c. flour, 1 egg and ¼ tsp. salt in top of double boiler. Cook until thick. Cool. Meanwhile, whip 2 c. heavy cream. Fold into cooled mixture.

## SPECIAL CHOCOLATE APPLE CAKE

*Chocolate and apple pair up to make an unusual and attractive cake*

| | |
|---|---|
| ½ c. butter | 2 tsp. baking powder |
| 2 c. sugar | ½ tsp. salt |
| 3 eggs | 1 c. milk |
| 3 c. sifted flour | 1 c. finely chopped peeled |
| ½ c. cocoa | apples |
| 1 tsp. ground cinnamon | Ambrosia Filling (recipe follows) |
| 1 tsp. ground nutmeg | |

Cream together butter and sugar until light and fluffy. Add eggs, one at a time, beating well after each addition.

Sift together dry ingredients; add alternately with milk to creamed mixture. Stir in apples. Pour batter into 2 greased 9″ round layer cake pans.

Bake in moderate oven (350°) 35 minutes, or until cake tests done. Cool on racks. Spread Ambrosia Filling between layers and on top of cooled cake. Makes 10 to 12 servings.

**Ambrosia Filling:** Combine 1½ c. sugar and ¼ c. flour in 2-qt. saucepan. Add ¼ c. butter, 1 (3½ oz.) can flaked coconut, 1 c. chopped raisins (optional), 1 c. milk, 3 tsp. grated orange peel and ½ tsp. baking powder. Cook until thick, stirring constantly. Stir in 1 c. chopped walnuts and 1 tsp. vanilla. Cool before spreading on cake.

## COCOA CHIFFON CAKE

*The chocolate shadow effect makes this a most elegant-looking cake*

| | |
|---|---|
| ½ c. cocoa | 1¾ c. sugar |
| ¾ c. boiling water | 1½ tsp. baking soda |
| 8 eggs, separated | 1 tsp. salt |
| ½ tsp. cream of tartar | ½ c. salad oil |
| 1¾ c. sifted cake flour | 2 tsp. vanilla |

Combine cocoa and boiling water.

Beat egg whites with cream of tartar until very stiff peaks form.

Sift together cake flour, sugar, baking soda and salt into a mixing bowl. Make a well in the center. Add oil, egg yolks, cocoa mixture and vanilla; beat well. Fold in egg whites, blend well. Pour into an ungreased 10″ tube pan. Cut through batter with spatula. Bake in slow oven (325°) 55 minutes. Increase temperature to moderate (350°) and bake 10 minutes longer, or until cake tests done. Invert to cool. Frost with your favorite chocolate frosting.

If you wish, decorate edges with chocolate shadow made by melting together 2 squares unsweetened chocolate and 2 tsp. butter over low heat. Cool slightly. Spoon along edge of frosted cake allowing chocolate to drip down sides. Makes 10 to 12 servings.

## FUDGE RIBBON CAKE

*There is a surprise cheese layer in this rich chocolate cake*

| | |
|---|---|
| 2 tblsp. butter | 1 tsp. baking powder |
| ¼ c. sugar | ½ tsp. baking soda |
| 1 tblsp. cornstarch | ½ c. shortening |
| 1 (8 oz.) pkg. cream cheese | 1½ c. milk |
| 1 egg | 2 eggs |
| 2 tblsp. milk | 4 squares unsweetened |
| ½ tsp. vanilla | chocolate, melted |
| 2 c. sifted flour | 1 tsp. vanilla |
| 2 c. sugar | Easy Chocolate Frosting (recipe |
| 1 tsp. salt | follows) |

Cream together butter, ¼ c. sugar and cornstarch. Add cheese and beat until fluffy. Add 1 egg, 2 tblsp. milk and ½ tsp. vanilla; beat until creamy. Set aside.

To make cake batter, combine flour, 2 c. sugar, salt, baking powder and soda. Add shortening and 1 c. milk; blend at lowest speed of mixer. Beat 1½ minutes at low speed or 225 strokes by hand. Add 2 eggs, chocolate, 1 tsp. vanilla and ½ c. milk; continue beating 1½ minutes at low speed.

Grease and flour bottom of 13×9×2″ pan.

Spread half of batter in pan. Spoon on cheese mixture, spreading carefully to cover batter. Top with remaining batter; spread to cover. Bake in moderate oven (350°) 50 to 55 minutes, until cake springs back when touched lightly in center. Cool on rack, then frost with Easy Chocolate Frosting. Makes 10 to 12 servings.

**Easy Chocolate Frosting:** Bring ⅓ c. milk and ¼ c. butter to a boil; remove from heat. Blend in 1 (6 oz.) pkg. semisweet chocolate pieces. Stir in 1 tsp. vanilla and 2¼ c. sifted confectioners sugar.

## FAVORITE FUDGE CAKE

*Luscious cake, but fragile. Handle gently when filling and frosting*

| | |
|---|---|
| ¾ c. butter or regular margarine | 3 c. sifted cake flour |
| 2¼ c. sugar | 1½ tsp. baking soda |
| 1½ tsp. vanilla | ¾ tsp. salt |
| 3 eggs | 1½ c. ice water |
| 3 squares unsweetened chocolate, melted | Date Cream Filling (recipe follows) |
| | Fudge Frosting (recipe follows) |

Cream together butter, sugar and vanilla. Add eggs, beating until light and fluffy. Add melted chocolate and blend well.

Sift together dry ingredients; add alternately with water to chocolate mixture. Pour batter into three 8″ round layer cake pans which have been greased and lined with waxed paper.

Bake in moderate oven (350°) 30 to 35 minutes. Cool on racks. Put layers together with Date Cream Filling. Frost with Fudge Frosting, spreading on sides of cake first and a little over the top edge. Frost top last. Makes 10 to 12 servings.

**Date Cream Filling:** Combine 1 c. milk and ½ c. chopped dates in top of double boiler.

Combine 1 tblsp. flour and ¼ c. sugar; add 1 beaten egg, blending until smooth. Add to hot milk mixture. Cook, stirring, until thick. Cool.

Stir in ½ c. chopped nuts and 1 tsp. vanilla. Spread between layers.

**Fudge Frosting:** Combine 2 c. sugar, ¼ tsp. salt, 1 c. light cream, 2 tblsp. light corn syrup and 2 squares unsweetened chocolate. Cook over low heat, stirring until sugar dissolves. Cover saucepan for 2 or 3 minutes. Remove lid and cook to the soft ball stage (234°). Beat to a spreading consistency. Add a little hot water if frosting becomes too stiff to spread evenly, sifted confectioners sugar if too thin. Frosts sides and top of three 8″ layers.

## FUDGE/LEMON CAKE

*The tangy lemon flavor enhances this rich chocolate fudge layer cake*

| | |
|---|---|
| ½ c. soft butter | 1 tsp. salt |
| 2 c. sugar | 2 tsp. baking powder |
| 4 eggs | 1¼ c. milk |
| 4 squares unsweetened | 2 tsp. vanilla |
|    chocolate, melted | Chocolate/Lemon Frosting |
| 2 c. sifted flour |    (recipe follows) |

Cream butter and sugar until light and fluffy. Beat in eggs, one at a time. Add melted chocolate and blend.

Sift dry ingredients together; add alternately with milk and vanilla to the creamed mixture.

Grease the sides of three 9″ round layer cake pans; dust with cocoa. Line bottoms of pans with ungreased paper. Divide batter evenly between the pans.

Bake in moderate oven (350°) about 30 minutes, or until the cake is done.

Cool on wire racks about 5 minutes; remove from pans and cool completely on racks. Spread Chocolate/Lemon Frosting between cake layers and on top of cake. Decorate with shaved chocolate pieces, if you wish. Makes 12 to 16 servings.

**Chocolate/Lemon Frosting:** Cream ½ c. butter with 1 c. sifted confectioners sugar, 3 squares sweet cooking chocolate, melted, and 1 egg. Add 3 c. sifted confectioners sugar, 1 tsp. vanilla (optional), ¼ tsp. salt and grated peel of 1 lemon (about 1 tblsp.). Beat until smooth. If frosting is too thick to spread, add a little milk. Stir in 1 c. chopped nuts.

## EXQUISITE COCONUT CAKE

*The yellow lemon filling is the highlight of this delicious cake*

| | |
|---|---|
| 2¼ c. sifted cake flour | 1 tsp. vanilla |
| 1½ c. sugar | 4 egg whites |
| 3½ tsp. baking powder | Lemon Filling (recipe follows) |
| 1 tsp. salt | 7-Minute Frosting (recipe follows) |
| ½ c. shortening | Shredded coconut |
| 1 c. milk | |

Sift together flour, sugar, baking powder and salt in large bowl. Add shortening, ⅔ c. milk and vanilla. Beat 2 minutes at high speed, scraping bowl occasionally. Add remaining milk and egg whites. Beat 2 minutes more, scraping bowl occasionally. Pour into 2 greased and floured 9″ round layer cake pans. Bake in moderate oven (350°) 30 minutes, or until done. Cool on racks.

When cool, put layers together with Lemon Filling. Frost sides and top of cake with 7-Minute Frosting, sprinkle with coconut. Makes 10 to 12 servings.

**Lemon Filling:** In small saucepan, combine ¾ c. sugar, 3 tblsp. cornstarch and ¼ tsp. salt. Stir in ¾ c. water. Cook, stirring constantly, until mixture thickens and boils; cook 1 minute. Remove from heat. Blend in 1 tblsp. butter, 1 tsp. grated lemon peel, ⅓ c. lemon juice and 4 drops yellow food color. Cool thoroughly.

**7-Minute Frosting:** In double boiler, combine 1 egg white, ¾ c. sugar, ⅛ tsp. cream of tartar (or 1½ tsp. light corn syrup) and 3 tblsp. water. Place over boiling water and beat until mixture stands in stiff peaks. Scrape bottom and sides of pan occasionally. Makes enough to frost two 8 or 9″ layers.

## CITRUS LAYER CAKE

*Double citrus flavor—both orange and lemon—makes this different*

| | |
|---|---|
| 2 eggs, separated | 1 c. milk |
| ½ c. sugar | 1 tsp. vanilla |
| 2 c. plus 2 tblsp. sifted flour | ½ tsp. orange extract |
| 1 tblsp. baking powder | Lemon Butter Filling (recipe |
| 1 tsp. salt | follows) |
| 1 c. sugar | Orange Butter Frosting (recipe |
| ⅓ c. salad oil | follows) |

Beat egg whites until frothy. Beat in ½ c. sugar; beat until stiff peaks form.

Sift together flour, baking powder, salt and 1 c. sugar. Add oil, ¾ c. milk and flavorings. Beat 1 minute at medium speed.

Add remaining milk and egg yolks, beat 1 minute. Fold in egg whites. Place in 2 greased and waxed paper-lined 9″ round layer cake pans. Bake in moderate oven (350°) 25 to 30 minutes.

Cool 10 minutes in pan before removing to rack. Put layers

together with Lemon Butter Filling and frost top and sides of cake with Orange Butter Frosting. Makes 12 servings.

**Lemon Butter Filling:** Combine in saucepan: 1 egg, ⅔ c. sugar, grated peel of 1 lemon, 2 tblsp. plus 2 tsp. lemon juice and 3 tblsp. butter. Cook over low heat 10 minutes, stirring constantly until mixture thickens. Cool before spreading between cake layers.

**Orange Butter Frosting:** Combine ⅓ c. butter, 1 lb. confectioners sugar, sifted, ⅛ tsp. salt and ½ tsp. orange extract. Add 4 to 6 tblsp. light cream, beating constantly until light and fluffy.

## BLACK WALNUT CAKE

*Serve this attractive cake at a women's luncheon or bridge party*

| | |
|---|---|
| 1 c. flaked coconut | ½ c. shortening |
| ⅓ c. black walnuts | ½ tsp. vanilla |
| ¼ c. chopped black walnuts | ½ tsp. maple flavoring |
| 2¼ c. sifted flour | 2 eggs |
| 1 tsp. baking powder | 1 c. buttermilk |
| 1 tsp. baking soda | ⅓ c. hot strong coffee |
| 1 tsp. salt | Creamy Coffee Icing (recipe |
| 1 c. sugar | follows) |

Grind together coconut and ⅓ c. black walnuts; add the chopped black walnuts. Set aside.

Sift together flour, baking powder, soda and salt; set aside.

Cream together sugar and shortening; add vanilla and maple flavoring. Add eggs, one at a time, beating well after each addition. Add dry ingredients alternately with buttermilk. Stir in coffee and all but 2 tblsp. coconut-nut mixture. Blend thoroughly. Turn into 2 greased and floured 9″ round layer cake pans. Bake in moderate oven (375°) 30 to 35 minutes, or until cake tests done. Spread Creamy Coffee Icing between layers and on top and sides of cake. Sprinkle top with reserved coconut-nut mixture. Makes 10 to 12 servings.

**Creamy Coffee Icing:** Cream together 4 c. sifted confectioners sugar and ¼ c. shortening. Add ½ tsp. maple flavoring, ½ tsp. vanilla and dash of salt. Beat in 2 tblsp. melted butter and enough hot strong coffee (2 to 3 tblsp.) to make frosting of spreading consistency.

## COCONUT/PECAN CAKE

*Studded with pecans . . . one of the best cakes we've ever tasted*

| | |
|---|---|
| 1 c. butter | ½ tsp. salt |
| ½ c. shortening | 1 c. buttermilk |
| 2 c. sugar | 1 (3½ oz.) can flaked coconut |
| 5 eggs | (1⅓ c.) |
| 1½ tsp. vanilla | 1 c. chopped pecans |
| 2 c. sifted flour | 1 tblsp. flour |
| 1 tsp. baking soda | Creamy Icing (recipe follows) |

Cream together butter, shortening and sugar until light and fluffy. Add eggs, one at a time, beating well. Add vanilla.

Sift together flour, baking soda and salt. Add alternately with buttermilk to creamed mixture, blend well. Mix coconut and pecans with 1 tblsp. flour and stir in.

Pour into 2 greased and floured 9″ round layer cake pans. Bake in moderate oven (350°) for 25 to 30 minutes. Cool. Frost layers, sides and top of cake with Creamy Icing. Makes 12 servings.

**Creamy Icing:** Combine 1 (8 oz.) pkg. softened cream cheese, 1 (1 lb.) pkg. confectioners sugar, 1 tblsp. milk and 1½ tsp. vanilla. Beat until smooth.

## BOSTON CREAM PIE

*Cinderella of American desserts—plain cake in glamorous dress*

| | |
|---|---|
| 2 c. sifted cake flour | 1 tsp. vanilla |
| 1¼ c. sugar | ¼ tsp. almond extract (optional) |
| 2½ tsp. baking powder | 1 egg, unbeaten |
| 1 tsp. salt | Custard Cream Filling (recipe |
| ⅓ c. shortening | follows) |
| 1 c. milk | Chocolate Icing (recipe follows) |

Sift dry ingredients into mixing bowl. Add shortening, milk, vanilla and almond extract. Beat 2 minutes, using medium speed on electric mixer, or 300 strokes by hand.

Add egg; beat 2 minutes more. Pour into 2 greased 8 or 9″ round layer cake pans.

Bake in moderate oven (350°) 25 to 30 minutes. Cool on

racks. Use one layer to make Boston Cream Pie; freeze the other for use later.

Split cooled cake layer in crosswise halves. Spread Custard Cream Filling over lower half. Cover with top half. Dust with confectioners sugar. Or spread with Chocolate Icing. Makes 6 servings.

## CUSTARD CREAM FILLING

*Smooth as velvet and one of the great delicacies of country kitchens*

| | |
|---|---|
| 1 c. milk, scalded | 2 eggs, slightly beaten |
| ½ c. sugar | 1 tblsp. butter or regular |
| 3 tblsp. cornstarch | margarine |
| ⅛ tsp. salt | 1 tsp. vanilla |

Gradually add milk to mixture of sugar, cornstarch and salt. Cook slowly, stirring constantly, until mixture thickens, about 10 to 15 minutes.

Add about ½ c. hot mixture to eggs and blend; carefully combine both mixtures and cook about 3 minutes, stirring constantly.

Remove from heat; blend in butter and vanilla. Cool. Makes 1¼ cups.

**Chocolate Icing:** Blend together 2 tblsp. butter or shortening, 2 squares unsweetened chocolate, melted, ¼ tsp. salt and ½ tsp. vanilla. Add 2¼ c. sifted confectioners sugar alternately with ¼ to ⅓ c. milk; beat until smooth. If thinner glaze is desired, add a little more milk.

## *Variations*

**Banana Custard Cream Filling:** Spread custard filling between halves of split cake layer. Cover custard with banana slices (1 medium to large banana, sliced and sprinkled with lemon juice) and top with remaining cake.

**Pineapple Custard Cream Filling:** Combine 1 c. cooled filling with ½ c. drained crushed pineapple just before spreading between split cake. Pineapple may also be added to all the following variations.

**Orange/Pineapple Custard Cream Filling:** Add 1 tsp. grated orange peel to pineapple filling.

**Coconut Custard Cream Filling:** Add ⅔ c. flaked or cut shredded coconut to custard filling.

## LUSCIOUS BUTTERMILK CAKE

*Lemon-Butter-Egg Sauce highlights this country-style cake*

| | |
|---|---|
| 1 c. shortening | 1 tsp. baking powder |
| 2¼ c. sugar | ½ tsp. baking soda |
| 2 tsp. vanilla | 1 tsp. salt |
| 1 tblsp. lemon juice | ¾ c. buttermilk |
| 1 tsp. grated lemon peel | Lemon-Butter-Egg Sauce (recipe |
| 6 eggs, separated | follows) |
| 3 c. sifted flour | |

Beat together shortening and 1½ c. sugar. Blend in vanilla, lemon juice and peel. Add egg yolks, one at a time, blending just until smooth after each addition.

Sift together flour, baking powder, baking soda and salt. Add alternately with buttermilk to first mixture, blending until smooth.

Beat egg whites until frothy, then gradually beat in remaining ¾ c. sugar until egg whites stand in stiff peaks. Fold into batter.

Spoon batter into 10″ tube pan that has been greased and dusted with fine bread crumbs. Bake in moderate oven (350°) about 1 hour and 15 minutes, or until cake tests done. Cool on rack. Makes 16 servings.

**Lemon-Butter-Egg Sauce:** In a small saucepan, combine ½ c. butter or margarine, 1 c. sugar, ¼ c. water, 1 well-beaten egg and 3 tblsp. lemon juice. Cook over medium heat, stirring constantly, just until mixture comes to a boil. Makes about 1½ cups.

## BLUE RIBBON BANANA CAKE

*Coconut baked on batter gives cake its characteristic crunchy top*

| | |
|---|---|
| ¾ c. shortening | ½ c. buttermilk |
| 1½ c. sugar | 1 tsp. vanilla |
| 2 eggs | ½ c. chopped pecans |
| 1 c. mashed bananas | 1 c. flaked coconut |
| ½ tsp. salt | Creamy Nut Filling (recipe |
| 2 c. sifted cake flour | follows) |
| 1 tsp. baking soda | White Snow Frosting (recipe |
| 1 tsp. baking powder | follows) |

Cream together shortening and sugar until fluffy. Add eggs; beat 2 minutes at medium speed. Add mashed bananas. Beat 2 minutes.

Sift together dry ingredients. Add to creamed mixture along with buttermilk and vanilla. Beat 2 minutes. Stir in nuts.

Turn into 2 greased and floured 9" round layer cake pans. Sprinkle ½ c. coconut on each layer. Bake in a moderate oven (375°) 25 to 30 minutes. Remove from pans. Cool layers, coconut side up, on racks.

Place first layer, coconut side down, and spread on Creamy Nut Filling. Top with second layer, coconut side up. Swirl White Snow Frosting around sides and about 1" around top edge, leaving center unfrosted. Makes 10 to 12 servings.

**Creamy Nut Filling:** Combine ½ c. sugar, 2 tblsp. flour, ½ c. cream and 2 tblsp. butter in heavy saucepan. Cook until thickened. Add ½ c. chopped pecans, ¼ tsp. salt and 1 tsp. vanilla. Cool.

**White Snow Frosting:** Cream together 1 egg white, ¼ c. shortening, ¼ c. butter, ½ tsp. coconut extract and ½ tsp. vanilla until well blended. Gradually add 2 c. sifted confectioners sugar, beating until light and fluffy.

## DEEP SOUTH FIG CAKE

*Serve this Southern delicacy with a scoop of vanilla ice cream*

| | |
|---|---|
| ½ c. butter | ½ c. buttermilk |
| 1 c. sugar | ½ c. fig juice |
| 2 eggs | 1 tsp. vanilla |
| 2 c. sifted flour | 1 qt. canned or 2 (1 lb. 1 oz.) |
| 1 tsp. salt | jars figs, drained and chopped |
| 1 tsp. baking powder | 1 c. chopped pecans |
| ½ tsp. baking soda | Fig Filling (recipe follows) |
| ½ tsp. ground cinnamon | Caramel Frosting (recipe |
| ¼ tsp. ground cloves | follows) |

Cream together butter and sugar until light and fluffy. Beat in eggs.

Sift together dry ingredients. Combine buttermilk and fig juice and add alternately with dry ingredients to creamed mixture. Beat until smooth.

Add vanilla and fold in figs, reserving ⅔ c. to use in the filling. Stir in pecans.

Pour batter into 2 greased 8" round layer cake pans. Bake in slow oven (325°) 1 hour, or until cake tests done. Remove from oven, cool in pan 10 minutes, then invert cake layers on racks and cool completely. Put together with Fig Filling and frost with Caramel Frosting. Makes 8 servings.

**Fig Filling:** Cook 1½ tsp. cornstarch with ⅓ c. fig juice until mixture is clear. Fold in ⅔ c. chopped and drained figs. Spread between layers.

**Caramel Frosting:** Melt ½ c. butter; add 1 c. dark brown sugar, firmly packed. Boil over low heat 2 minutes, stirring; add ¼ c. milk. Bring to boil; cool; add 1¾ c. sifted confectioners sugar. Cool, beat.

## CHOCOLATE CAKE RING

*Fudge and black walnut flavors make this an unforgettable cake*

| | |
|---|---|
| 2¼ c. sifted cake flour | ⅔ c. shortening |
| 1¾ c. sugar | 2 tsp. vanilla |
| 1 tsp. baking soda | ⅔ c. buttermilk |
| ½ tsp. baking powder | 4 eggs |
| 1½ tsp. salt | 1½ c. black walnuts, finely |
| 3 squares unsweetened chocolate | chopped |
| ½ c. boiling water | Fudge Frosting (recipe follows) |

Sift together dry ingredients.

Cut chocolate into fine pieces in mixing bowl. Pour on boiling water. Let stand until soft; blend. Add shortening and vanilla; beat smooth.

Add all but ¼ c. buttermilk and dry ingredients. Blend at low speed, then beat 2 minutes with mixer or 300 strokes by hand.

Add eggs and remaining buttermilk; blend together. Beat 2 minutes more. Fold in nuts. Pour into greased and floured 3-qt. ring mold.

Bake in moderate oven (350°) 35 to 40 minutes, or until cake tests done. Cool 5 minutes; turn out on rack. Frost, bottom side up, with Fudge Frosting. Makes 16 servings.

**Fudge Frosting:** Cut 2 squares unsweetened chocolate into pieces. Combine with 1¾ c. sugar, 1 tblsp. light corn syrup, ½ c. milk, 6 tblsp. butter or regular margarine and ¼ tsp. salt in 2-qt. saucepan. Mix well. Place over heat; bring to full rolling boil. Boil 2 minutes, stirring constantly. Remove from heat; let cool to lukewarm. Add 1 tsp. vanilla. Beat until of spreading consistency.

## WALNUT CAKE RING

*A recipe to treasure—tender white cake loaded with walnuts*

| | |
|---|---|
| 3¾ c. sifted cake flour | 2 tsp. vanilla |
| 2 c. sugar | 1¼ c. milk |
| 4 tsp. baking powder | 6 egg whites (¾ c.) |
| 1½ tsp. salt | 1½ c. walnuts, finely chopped |
| ½ c. soft butter | Creamy White Frosting (recipe |
| ½ c. shortening | follows) |

Sift together flour, sugar, baking powder and salt.

Blend together butter, shortening and vanilla. Add dry ingredients and 1 c. milk. Blend together at low speed on mixer, then beat 2 minutes with mixer or 300 strokes by hand.

Blend in remaining milk and egg whites. Beat 2 minutes. Fold in nuts. Pour into greased and floured 3-qt. ring mold.

Bake in moderate oven (350°) 35 to 40 minutes, or until cake tests done. Cool 5 minutes; turn out on rack. Frost, bottom side up, with Creamy White Frosting. Makes 16 servings.

**Creamy White Frosting:** Combine 3½ c. confectioners sugar, ½ c. soft butter or regular margarine, ¼ c. milk, ⅛ tsp. salt and 1 tsp. vanilla in mixing bowl. Blend, then beat until smooth. Add milk as needed (1 to 2 tblsp.) for frosting of good spreading consistency.

## AUTUMN FESTIVAL CAKE

*A marvelous apple cake—ideal to have on hand for Thanksgiving house guests. Crisp topping bakes with cake*

| | |
|---|---|
| 1 c. butter | 1 tsp. salt |
| ¾ c. brown sugar, firmly packed | 2 tsp. ground nutmeg |
| ¾ c. sugar | ½ tsp. ground mace |
| 4 eggs | 1 c. chopped walnuts |
| 1 c. grated peeled apples | 1 c. raisins |
| 1½ tsp. vanilla | 1 tblsp. flour |
| 1½ tsp. almond extract | ¼ c. chopped walnuts |
| 2½ c. sifted flour | 2 tblsp. brown sugar |
| 1½ tsp. baking powder | |

Cream butter and sugars together until light and fluffy. Beat in eggs, one at a time. Beat in apples and flavorings.

Sift together 2½ c. flour, baking powder, salt, nutmeg and mace; gradually blend into apple mixture.

Combine 1 c. walnuts, raisins and 1 tblsp. flour, and mix into batter.

Spoon into well-greased 9″ tube pan. Combine ¼ c. walnuts and 2 tblsp. brown sugar; sprinkle over the batter. Bake in slow oven (325°) 1 hour and 30 minutes.

Remove from oven, set pan on rack and let cake cool 15 minutes. Remove cake from pan and set on rack to cool completely. Makes 10 servings.


## MAPLE/DATE CAKE

*Keep this luscious dessert on hand to serve guests with coffee*

| | |
|---|---|
| 2 tsp. baking soda | 2 eggs, well beaten |
| 3 c. pitted, chopped dates | 1 tsp. salt |
| 2 c. boiling water | 2 c. sifted flour |
| 2 c. sugar | 3 tsp. maple flavoring |
| ¾ c. butter | 1 c. chopped nuts, floured |

Sprinkle soda over dates. Add water and mix.

Cream sugar with butter; mix in eggs, salt and flour. Add to date mixture. Blend in flavoring and nuts. (If you prefer a less pronounced maple taste, use 1 tsp. flavoring.)

Pour into greased 13×9×2″ pan. Bake in hot oven (400°) 15 minutes or until cake begins to brown; lower heat to slow (325°) and bake 35 minutes more.

Serve sliced, warm or cold, plain or with whipped cream flavored with lemon extract. Makes 18 servings.

## ROCKY MOUNTAIN CAKE

*A special spice cake baked in a tube pan with a brown sugar icing*

| | |
|---|---|
| 2 c. sifted flour | 7 eggs, separated |
| 1½ c. sugar | 2 tblsp. caraway seeds |
| 1 tblsp. baking powder | ½ c. salad oil |
| 1 tsp. salt | ¾ c. ice water |
| 1 tsp. ground cinnamon | ½ tsp. cream of tartar |
| ½ tsp. ground nutmeg | Rocky Mountain Frosting |
| ½ tsp. ground allspice | (recipe follows) |
| ½ tsp. ground cloves | |

Sift flour, sugar, baking powder, salt and spices together several times.

Combine egg yolks, caraway seeds, oil and water in large bowl. Add dry ingredients. Beat about ½ minute at low speed on mixer or 75 strokes by hand. (Add a few drops of lemon extract for different flavor.)

Add cream of tartar to egg whites. Beat until stiff peaks form.

Gradually pour egg yolk mixture over beaten whites; gently fold in.

Pour into ungreased 10″ tube pan. Bake in slow oven (325°) 55 minutes, then increase heat to moderate (350°) and bake 10 to 15 minutes more.

Invert pan on rack to cool cake. When completely cool, spread Rocky Mountain Frosting over top and sides of cake. Makes 10 to 12 servings.

**Rocky Mountain Frosting:** In saucepan, blend ½ c. butter with 2½ tblsp. flour and ¼ tsp. salt. Cook 1 minute; do not brown. Add ½ c. milk; cook until thick. While hot, add ½ c. brown sugar, firmly packed; beat well. Add 2 c. confectioners sugar, sifted; beat until thick and creamy. Add 1 tsp. vanilla and 1 c. chopped black walnuts, or other nuts.

## ORANGE BUTTER CAKE

*Pineapple filling goes between the layers and on top of this beauty*

| | |
|---|---|
| 1 c. soft butter (room temperature) | ½ tsp. salt |
| 2 c. sugar | 1 c. milk |
| 4 eggs | ¼ c. orange juice |
| 3 c. sifted flour | 1 tsp. vanilla |
| 3 tsp. baking powder | 1 tblsp. grated orange peel |
| ¼ tsp. baking soda | Pineapple Filling (recipe follows) |
| | 1 c. heavy cream, whipped |

Cream butter and sugar; beat in eggs one at a time.

Sift dry ingredients together; add alternately with the remaining ingredients, except filling, to creamed mixture. (Do not pour orange juice and milk into the same cup.)

Pour batter into three 9″ paper-lined round layer cake pans. Bake in moderate oven (350°) about 35 minutes.

Cool on racks about 5 minutes before removing from pans; complete cooling on wire racks. Put cooled layers together with Pineapple Filling. Spread filling on top of cake. Frost the sides with whipped cream. Makes 10 to 12 servings.

**Pineapple Filling:** Combine ¼ c. cornstarch, 1 c. sugar and 3 tblsp. orange juice in saucepan. Stir in 1 tsp. grated orange peel, ½ c. butter and 1 (1 lb. 4 oz.) can crushed pineapple, undrained. Cook over low heat until thick and glossy, stirring constantly. Cool before spreading on cake.

## SNOWDRIFT MARDI GRAS CAKE

*You can bake this glamorous cake the day before your party*

| | |
|---|---|
| 1 c. butter | 2¼ c. sifted cake flour |
| 1 (8 oz.) pkg. cream cheese, softened | 2 tsp. baking powder |
| 1½ c. sugar | ¼ c. sifted cake flour |
| 1½ tsp. vanilla | 2 c. mixed candied fruit (1 lb.) |
| 4 eggs | ½ c. coarsely chopped pecans |
| | ½ c. finely chopped pecans |

Thoroughly blend butter, softened cream cheese, sugar and vanilla. Add eggs, one at a time, beating well after each addition.

Sift together 2¼ c. sifted cake flour and baking powder. Add to batter and blend well.

Combine ¼ c. cake flour with candied fruit and ½ c. coarsely chopped pecans. Fold into batter. Spoon batter into a 10″ bundt or tube pan that has been greased and sprinkled with ½ c. finely chopped pecans.

Bake in slow oven (325°) 70 to 80 minutes, or until cake tests done. Cool in pan 5 minutes. Remove from pan; cool on rack.

Sprinkle with sifted confectioners sugar. Garnish with candied cherries and candied pineapple if you wish. Makes 16 servings.

## GRAND CHAMPION SPONGE CAKE

*We added the Creamy Pineapple Frosting for a special party look*

| | |
|---|---|
| 1¼ c. sifted flour | ½ c. sugar |
| 1 c. sugar | 6 egg yolks |
| ½ tsp. baking powder | ¼ c. water |
| ½ tsp. salt | 1 tsp. vanilla |
| 6 egg whites | Creamy Pineapple Frosting |
| 1 tsp. cream of tartar | (recipe follows) |

Sift together flour, 1 c. sugar, baking powder and salt.

In a large mixing bowl, beat egg whites until frothy. Add cream of tartar. Gradually beat in ½ c. sugar, a little at a time, beat until whites form stiff, not dry peaks.

In a small bowl, combine egg yolks, water, vanilla and sifted dry ingredients. Beat at medium high speed for 4 minutes or until mixture is light and fluffy. Fold yolk mixture gently, but thoroughly into the beaten egg whites. Turn into an ungreased 10″ tube pan. Bake in moderate oven (350°) about 45 minutes. Invert pan on rack to cool. Frost with Creamy Pineapple Frosting. Makes 10 to 12 servings.

**Creamy Pineapple Frosting:** Cream together ¼ c. butter and ¼ c. shortening. Gradually add 3 c. sifted confectioners sugar; beat until light and fluffy. Blend in 1 (8½ oz.) can crushed pineapple, drained, ⅛ tsp. salt, ¼ tsp. vanilla and ½ tsp. grated lemon peel.

## JUBILEE CAKE

*A country hostess special—sponge cake with crown of gold*

1 (10″) Country Sponge Cake
(recipe follows)
1 c. Pear Jubilee (recipe
follows)

1 c. heavy cream
3 tblsp. confectioners sugar

Remove cooled cake from pan and turn upside down. Spread top with Pear Jubilee.

Whip cream and blend in confectioners sugar. Spread on sides of cake. Cut into servings with a cake breaker or carefully pull in wedges with two forks. Serve the same day. Makes 12 servings.

### Pear Jubilee:

1 c. dried apricots, cut in thin
strips
1 lemon, cut in thin slices
¾ c. water

5 c. peeled, cored and finely
diced fresh pears
4 c. sugar
1 tblsp. rum extract

Combine apricots, lemon and water in saucepan. Cover; simmer 5 minutes and set aside.

Combine pears and sugar in heavy 4-qt. kettle. Cook over low heat until clear and thick, about 1 hour. Stir often to prevent scorching. Add apricot mixture; stir well. Add rum extract.

Ladle into hot sterilized jars. Seal. Makes 4 half-pints.

## COUNTRY SPONGE CAKE

*Use this feather-light, high cake for Jubilee Cake, or serve plain*

6 egg yolks
½ c. cold water
1½ c. sugar
½ tsp. vanilla
½ tsp. lemon extract

1½ c. sifted cake flour
¼ tsp. salt
6 egg whites
¾ tsp. cream of tartar

Beat egg yolks until thick and lemon-colored. Add water and beat until very thick. Gradually beat in the sugar. Add the vanilla and lemon extract.

Sift together flour and salt; fold into the egg yolk mixture, a little at a time.

Beat egg whites with cream of tartar until stiff peaks form. Pour the egg yolk batter over the egg whites and, with a rubber scraper, fold it into the whites, just to blend. Use an over and under motion, turning the bowl gradually.

Spoon into a 10″ ungreased tube pan. Bake in slow oven (325°) about 1 hour, or until cake tester or wooden pick, inserted halfway between center and side, comes out clean.

Invert and cool completely. It will take about 1½ hours. Loosen cake with spatula and remove from pan. Makes 12 servings.

N O T E : You can omit lemon extract and use 1 tsp. vanilla. Or use orange extract instead of lemon extract, especially good when cake's top wears Pear Jubilee.

## LADY BALTIMORE CAKE

*Simplified version of an elegant Dixie dessert—tastes wonderful*

| | |
|---|---|
| 1 (18½ oz.) pkg. white cake mix | ¼ c. chopped dates |
| | ½ c. chopped seeded raisins |
| 1 (14 oz.) pkg. white frosting mix | 12 candied cherries, chopped |
| | ½ c. chopped pecans |
| ¼ tsp. almond extract | |

Mix and bake cake as directed on package in two 8″ round or square layer cake pans. Cool.

Prepare frosting as directed on package, adding almond extract.

Combine ¾ c. frosting with fruits and nuts; spread between layers.

Frost top and side of cake with remaining frosting. Makes 10 servings.

N O T E : Substitute well-drained maraschino cherries for candied cherries. Use syrup from cherries as part of liquid in frosting to tint a delicate pink. Or, tint frosting with red food color.

## LORD BALTIMORE CAKE

*The Lady's companion—quick version of an old-time Dixie favorite*

1 (17 to 18½ oz.) pkg. yellow cake mix
1 (14 oz.) pkg. white frosting mix
¼ tsp. lemon or orange extract
¼ c. blanched chopped almonds
¼ c. chopped pecans
½ c. dry macaroon crumbs
12 candied cherries, chopped

Mix and bake cake as directed on package in two 8″ round layer cake pans. Cool.

Prepare frosting as directed on package, adding lemon extract.

Toast nuts and crumbs in moderate oven (350°) 5 minutes.

Blend nuts, crumbs and cherries into 1 c. frosting; spread between layers.

Frost top and side of cake with remaining frosting. Decorate side of cake with strips of candied cherries and nuts, if desired. Makes 10 servings.

## JELLY JEWEL CAKE

*Bits of bright red jelly sparkle in the smooth sour cream filling*

1 (18½ oz.) pkg. white cake mix
8 drops green food color (about)
12 drops yellow food color (about)
1 c. tart red jelly (currant, strawberry or raspberry)
2 c. dairy sour cream, or 2 c. heavy cream, whipped
3 medium bananas, thinly sliced
½ c. shredded coconut, fluffed

Prepare cake batter as directed on package; before last beating period divide batter in half.

Add green color to half the batter; yellow to other half. Finish beating.

Pour into four 8″ round layer cake pans. Bake as directed on package 10 minutes. Cool on racks.

Place ½ c. jelly in bowl; break in small pieces with fork; add sour cream, folding only 3 or 4 times.

Spread green layer with jelly mixture; top with sliced bananas. Repeat with yellow and other green layer. Top with yellow layer;

spread with remaining jelly, broken with fork; sprinkle coconut around edge. Makes 12 servings.


## ICELANDIC CAKE

*A traditional Yuletide cake filled with luscious prune filling*

| | |
|---|---|
| 1 c. butter | 1 tsp. ground cardamom |
| 1 c. sugar | ¼ tsp. salt |
| 3 eggs | ¼ c. milk |
| 3 c. sifted flour | Prune Filling (recipe follows) |
| 1½ tsp. baking powder | |

Cream together butter and sugar. Add eggs, one at a time, beating well after each addition.

Sift together flour, baking powder, cardamom and salt. Add to creamed mixture alternately with milk. Spread batter evenly in 4 greased 8″ round layer cake pans. Bake in moderate oven (350°) about 15 minutes, or until cakes test done. Cool on racks.

Spread Prune Filling between cooled layers. Let stand several days before serving. To serve, cut cake in crosswise slices ½″ thick. Makes 10 to 12 servings.

**Prune Filling:** Stir together 3 c. cooked pitted prunes (1 lb.) drained and puréed, 1 c. sugar, ½ tsp. ground cinnamon, ¼ tsp. ground nutmeg, ⅛ tsp. ground cloves and ⅛ tsp. salt. Spread between cooled cake layers.


## HOT MILK SPONGE CAKE

*Bits of maraschino cherries are hidden in the fluffy orange filling*

| | |
|---|---|
| 1 c. milk | 1¾ c. sugar |
| 2 tblsp. butter | 1 tsp. vanilla |
| 2 c. sifted flour | 1 tsp. lemon extract |
| 2 tsp. baking powder | Fluffy Orange Frosting (recipe |
| ½ tsp. salt | follows) |
| 4 eggs | |

Heat milk and butter until scalding.

Sift together flour, baking powder and salt; set aside.

Beat eggs well. Gradually beat in sugar, beating until thick and lemon-colored. Add vanilla and lemon extract. Beat in hot milk mixture. Beat in dry ingredients at low speed, mixing well. Pour into 3 waxed paper-lined 9″ round layer cake pans. Bake in moderate oven (350°) for 35 to 40 minutes or until cake tests done. Spread layers, sides and top of cake with Fluffy Orange Frosting. Makes 12 servings.

**Fluffy Orange Frosting:** Combine 2 egg whites, 1⅓ c. sugar, ⅓ c. light corn syrup, ¼ c. orange juice, 1 tsp. grated orange peel and ½ tsp. cream of tartar in the top of a double boiler. Beat constantly with electric mixer over simmering water for 5 minutes or until mixture thickens and is still glossy. Remove pan from heat. Spread frosting on first layer and sprinkle with 2 tblsp. chopped maraschino cherries. Repeat with next layer. Place third layer on top. Spread frosting on sides and top of cake.

## COCONUT CHIFFON CAKE

*A tender, light chiffon cake with coconut . . . perfect for birthdays*

| | |
|---|---|
| 8 egg whites | ½ c. salad oil |
| ½ tsp. cream of tartar | 8 egg yolks |
| 2 c. sifted flour | ¾ c. cold water |
| 1½ c. sugar | 1 tsp. vanilla |
| 3 tsp. baking powder | 1 (3½ oz.) can flaked coconut |
| 1 tsp. salt | (1⅓ c.) |

Beat egg whites with cream of tartar until stiff but not dry. Set aside.

Sift together flour, sugar, baking powder and salt into a large mixing bowl. Make a well in the center and add oil, egg yolks, water and vanilla. Beat well. Pour egg yolk mixture gradually over beaten egg whites and fold gently until blended (do not stir). Fold in coconut. Pour into ungreased 10″ tube pan. Bake in moderate oven (325°) for 50 to 55 minutes or until cake tests done. Makes 12 servings.

## CAKES TO MAKE THE DAY AHEAD

Here's a collection of cakes that can be assembled the day before company is coming. You can add glamor to homemade or supermarket cakes and frostings. The results look like you have spent hours in the kitchen fixing a fancy dessert.

### LEMON JELLY CAKE

*Yellow and white ribbon cake with lemon taste—good make-ahead*

1 (9 or 10") angel food cake
1 envelope unflavored gelatin
1½ c. sugar
4 tblsp. cornstarch
⅛ tsp. salt
⅓ c. water
2 egg yolks, beaten
2 tblsp. butter or regular margarine

¼ tsp. grated lemon peel
⅓ c. fresh lemon juice
½ c. dairy sour cream
½ c. chopped nuts
Lemon-Fluff Frosting (recipe follows)

Cut cool cake in 3 equal layers.

Combine gelatin with ¼ c. sugar and set aside.

Combine remaining 1¼ c. sugar, cornstarch and salt. Add water; cook over low heat, stirring constantly, until the mixture thickens and boils. Stir ½ c. hot mixture into egg yolks; stir this back into hot mixture. Return to heat and cook 1 minute, stirring constantly.

Remove from heat and add gelatin-sugar mixture. Stir until gelatin dissolves; stir in butter. Continue to stir until mixture starts to set but is still "soupy." Add lemon juice and peel; fold in sour cream and nuts. Cool. Spread between layers of cake. Frost top and side of cake with Lemon-Fluff Frosting. Makes 10 to 12 servings.

**Lemon-Fluff Frosting:** In double boiler, combine 1 egg white (2 tblsp.), ¾ c. sugar, ⅛ tsp. cream of tartar or 1½ tsp. light corn syrup and 3 tblsp. water. Place over boiling water and beat with rotary beater or electric mixer until mixture stands in stiff peaks. Scrape bottom and sides of pan occasionally. Fold in 2 tsp. grated lemon peel and tint a delicate yellow with food color. Spread on cake.

## EGG NOG CAKE

*A spectacular company dessert that can be made ahead and frozen*

¾ c. butter
2½ c. sifted confectioners sugar
4 egg yolks
¼ c. brandy or rum
1 c. toasted slivered almonds,
chopped

1 angel food cake, split into 3
layers
1 c. heavy cream
1 square semisweet chocolate,
shaved into thin curls

Cream butter; stir in sugar until well blended. Mix in egg yolks, one at a time, blending well. Gradually stir in brandy or rum; blend until smooth (do not beat). Fold in ¾ c. of the almonds.

Spread this mixture between layers of angel cake. Cover with waxed paper and chill 24 hours, or cover with foil and freeze.

Just before serving, whip heavy cream and frost top and sides of cake. Decorate top with remaining ¼ c. almonds and chocolate curls. Makes 16 servings.

## HAWAIIAN ANGEL CAKE

*Pastel pink and green fillings make this delectable cake glamorous*

1 (10″) angel food cake, split
in 3 layers
1 (1 lb. 13 oz.) can crushed
pineapple
2 envelopes unflavored gelatin
Peppermint extract
Green food color

2 envelopes dessert topping mix,
whipped according to package
directions
¾ c. drained and chopped
maraschino cherries
3 tblsp. maraschino cherry juice
Red food color

Drain pineapple well; reserve syrup. Soften gelatin in pineapple syrup; place over low heat until gelatin is melted. Mix with drained pineapple.

Remove ⅓ (about 1 c. plus 2 tblsp.) of pineapple mixture to separate bowl. Flavor this amount with a few drops of peppermint extract and color a delicate green. Fold in ⅓ of whipped topping mix.

To remainder of pineapple mixture, add chopped cherries and

cherry juice. Fold in the remaining whipped topping mix. Color pink.

Spread bottom layer of angel food cake with half of the pink cherry whip, add second layer and spread with green mint whip. Add top layer and spread with last of pink cherry whip. Leave sides of cake bare. Refrigerate 1 hour or more to firm. Makes 12 servings.

## MOCHA-FROSTED CAKE

*For hostesses who like to stay to visit with their guests*

1 (3¾ oz.) pkg. chocolate
    pudding and pie filling
1½ tblsp. instant coffee
1⅓ c. milk
1 c. heavy cream, whipped

1 (10″) angel food cake, split in
    three equal layers
2 (¾ oz.) chocolate-coated toffee
    bars, crushed

Blend pudding mix, coffee and milk. Prepare pudding as directed on package. Chill. Beat smooth; fold in half of the whipped cream. Spread half of the pudding mixture between the cake layers.

Fold second half of whipped cream into remaining pudding mixture. Spread on top and sides of cake. Sprinkle with crushed candy. Chill several hours before serving. Makes 12 servings.

NOTE: This cake freezes well. First, freeze it uncovered. When firm, wrap and return to freezer. To serve, place cake, uncovered, in refrigerator 3 hours to reach serving temperature.

## REFRIGERATOR DESSERT DE LUXE

*This lovely dessert is made the day ahead . . . no last-minute rush*

1½ lb. baked pound cake
1 (12 oz.) pkg. semisweet
    chocolate pieces
3 eggs, separated
1 tsp. vanilla
½ c. sugar
3 tblsp. milk

1 tblsp. sugar
1 (8 oz.) pkg. cream cheese
¼ tsp. salt
1 c. heavy cream
½ c. sugar
Whipped cream for garnish

Butter sides of loose-bottomed torte pan (9″ across, 3″ deep).

Line bottom of pan with several ¼″ cake slices; leave space around sides for cake strips. Place ½″ thick cake slices, about 3″

long, around sides of pan, spacing evenly (you will need 18 or 20). Use remaining cake to make a layer or two between filling.

Melt chocolate pieces over hot, not boiling, water. Cover, and let stand about 10 minutes.

Place egg whites in small bowl; beat until soft peaks form. Add vanilla; gradually add ½ c. sugar, beating until stiff peaks form. Set aside.

Mix yolks with milk and 1 tblsp. sugar. Add to chocolate; beat smooth with a spoon. Set aside to cool.

Place cheese (at room temperature) in large bowl. Add salt; mix until smooth. Add heavy cream and ½ c. sugar alternately; beat at medium speed. Mixture should stay thick and smooth.

Add cooled chocolate; mix at low speed. Mix in egg whites at low speed.

Pour a third of mixture into torte pan. Make a layer of cake pieces (keep side pieces in place). Repeat layers, ending with filling. If cake strips around edge are above filling, let cake set, then remove tips with sharp knife after cake is taken from pan. Chill 6 hours, or overnight.

To serve, remove pan sides; leave cake on pan bottom and place on serving plate. Garnish rim with whipped cream. Makes 16 servings.


## QUICK HOLIDAY CAKE

*Yuletide dessert gem: Plain cake with jeweled frosting on top*

| | |
|---|---|
| 2 tblsp. butter or regular margarine | ⅓ c. mixed candied fruit, chopped |
| ⅓ c. brown sugar, firmly packed | ⅓ c. broken nuts |
| 2 tblsp. evaporated milk | ⅓ c. flaked coconut |
| | 1 (8″) square baked cake layer |

Blend together butter, brown sugar and evaporated milk. Add fruit, nuts and coconut.

Put cake on baking sheet; spread fruit mixture over top. Place under preheated broiler until delicate brown and bubbly, about 2 to 3 minutes. Makes 9 to 12 servings.

## CRESTED DESSERT CAKE

*Use a cake from the freezer for this hot-from-the-oven treat*

1 (8 or 9") baked layer white
  or sponge cake
½ c. crunchy peanut butter

1 c. apricot jam
½ c. flaked or shredded coconut

Turn cake bottom side up on baking sheet. Spread with peanut butter, then with jam. (Or mix peanut butter with jam before spreading—it goes on easier.) Sprinkle with coconut.

Place cake in cold oven, then turn on heat and set temperature control at 350°. Turn off heat in 5 minutes. Leave cake in oven while first part of dinner is eaten. Cut in wedges. Makes 6 servings.

## *Variation*

**Raisin-Crested Dessert Cake:** Use raisins, rinsed in warm water and wiped dry with paper towel, instead of coconut. Raisins puff up in oven. For a company touch, top cake with scoops of vanilla ice cream.

# CHAPTER 8

# *Easy-Does-It Cake Decorating*

Everyone appreciates a specially decorated cake for a birthday party, wedding reception or shower. But many homemakers shrug away from decorating because they don't know how to use a decorating tube and frankly are much too busy to take the time to learn. "I just wish I had some easy directions for making a cake look fancy without having a lot of fuss," many women tell us.

Our decorating chapter is full of simple but creative suggestions for many special occasions or situations. Some of them will start you on your way to your own variations. Many of the decorating makings will already be on hand in your own kitchen or can be found in your supermarkets, candy shops and in the local "five and ten." With a good selection of assorted candies, plastic straws, animal crackers, unfilled sugar-type ice cream cones, jellies, decorating gel (this comes in small tubes and can be found in most supermarkets throughout the country), you will be able to turn out imaginatively decorated cakes. Besides, you'll have fun doing it!

Our Yellow Shadow Cake serves triple duty . . . beautiful for a shower, birthday or graduation party, and the decoration is simply gumdrops shaped into a miniature beautiful bouquet. The Jeweled Hobnail Cake is a sparkling beauty, and again colored gumdrops play the major decorating role along with shiny silver dragées. The children will want to help to decorate the Easter Ring filled with assorted jelly beans.

No decorating chapter would be complete without a wedding cake—we feature two that are easy to do yourself, yet charmingly individual.

## YELLOW SHADOW CAKE

*A delicate yellow glazed cake decorated with gumdrop roses makes a lovely centerpiece for a shower, Mother's Day or a special birthday*

| | |
|---|---|
| 1 (9") angel food cake | Yellow food color |
| 2 c. white frosting | 5 large white gumdrops |
| 1 (6.2 oz.) pkg. vanilla glaze mix | 2 large green gumdrops |

Frost sides and top of cake with white frosting; let set about 15 minutes.

Meanwhile, make glaze according to package directions. Tint a delicate yellow with food color. Carefully spoon glaze over cake, letting it drip down sides to create shadow effect.

On a well-sugared board, roll all gumdrops into long strips. Cut white strips in lengthwise halves, roll up to make 10 small roses. Place in groups of two around top of cake. Using tip of a sharp knife, cut green strips into leaves of various sizes. Place among flowers as desired.

## JEWELED HOBNAIL CAKE

*An attractive cake that is very simple to make. For a variation, use red and green gumdrops and serve during the Christmas holidays*

| | |
|---|---|
| 2 (8 or 9") round cake layers | 8 to 10 large yellow gumdrops |
| 2 c. white frosting | Silver dragées |
| 8 to 10 large gumdrops | |

Put cake layers together with white frosting, frost sides and top of cake.

Using a sharp knife dipped in hot water, cut each gumdrop into 3 crosswise slices. Place in rows, alternating orange and yellow, over top of cake. Place silver dragées in decorative pattern on top of each gumdrop slice, and if desired between rows of gumdrops.

## EASTER RING

*This lovely cake holds either jelly beans or chocolate eggs. Children will be especially delighted with the marshmallow chicks*

Green food color
1 tsp. water
1 (7 oz.) can shredded coconut
1 cake layer, made in 9″
  (6½ c.) ring mold

1½ c. white frosting
Jelly beans or foil-wrapped
  chocolate eggs
Marshmallow chicks

In a large jar dilute a few drops of food color in water. Add coconut; cover and shake until evenly colored.

Frost cake completely with white frosting. Cover with green coconut pressing gently to secure in frosting. Fill center with jelly beans. Place marshmallow chicks around edge of cake.

## HALLOWEEN CAKE

*This decorating idea is also perfect for cupcakes . . . just make small jack o' lantern silhouettes and proceed as for the large cake*

2 (8 or 9″) round cake layers
2 c. white frosting
Orange decorating sugar
1 ($1\frac{1}{16}$ oz.) tube chocolate
  flavor decorating gel

1 ($1\frac{1}{16}$ oz.) tube green color
  glossy decorating gel
Candy corn

Put cake layers together with white frosting; frost sides and top of cake.

Make jack o' lantern silhouette pattern from paper. Place on top of cake; sprinkle pattern with orange sugar. Remove pattern; press sugar lightly to secure in frosting.

Using chocolate gel, outline jack o' lantern, and make features for face. Using green gel, make stem on jack o' lantern. Press candy corn around top and bottom edge of sides of cake.

## CAROUSEL CAKE

*A perfect cake for a child's birthday. For a special touch, use decorated homemade animal cookies instead of animal crackers*

2 (8 or 9") round cake layers
2 c. chocolate frosting
Animal crackers

Plastic straws
Construction paper

Spread some of the frosting over one cake layer; top with remaining layer. Frost sides, then top of cake.

Circle sides of cake with a row of animal crackers. Place a second row of animal crackers around top outer edge of cake, inserting straws behind crackers.

Cut construction paper into a 7½" circle for 8" cake, 8½" for a 9" cake. Draw line from center of circle to outside edge; cut on this line. Overlap cut edges slightly to make a slight conical shape. Place on top of straws to form a canopy.

## VALENTINE OR SWEETHEART CAKE

*Surprise your Valentine with this delicate pink heart-shaped cake. This cake is also a lovely addition to a small bridal shower*

2 heart-shaped cake layers
2 c. pink frosting
4 large red gumdrops

16 small red gumdrops
4 large green gumdrops

Put cake layers together with pink frosting; frost sides and top of cake.

On a well-sugared board, roll all gumdrops into long strips. Roll up all red strips to make roses. Arrange the four large and a few small roses in decorative spray on top of cake. Place remaining small roses around bottom edge of cake. Using tip of a sharp knife, cut leaves of various sizes; place among flowers to complete spray and place around roses at edge of cake.

## TOY TRAIN BIRTHDAY CAKE

*Delight your little boy with this special birthday cake. The plastic toy train candle holders and others are readily available*

2 (8 or 9″) round cake layers
2 c. chocolate frosting
1 (4¼ oz.) tube decorating icing
in desired color

Novelty train candle holders
Candles

Put cake layers together with chocolate frosting; frost sides and top of cake.

Using plain decorating tip, write "Happy Birthday" on top of cake with decorating icing. Use star tip and decorate around top edge and sides of cake. Place train candle holders and candles on top.

## LEMON SURPRISE

*Need a birthday cake in a hurry . . . transform a plain purchased angel food cake into a lemon surprise . . . it's sure to please everyone*

1 (9″) angel food cake
1 c. lemon filling

2 c. lemon frosting
8 jellied lemon slices

Cut cake in half crosswise. Fill with lemon filling. Frost sides, then top of cake with lemon frosting. Cut jellied lemon slices in halves; place on top and around sides of cake.

## SHOWER OR ANNIVERSARY CAKE

*This decorating idea can be suited to most any season or occasion. Use a cookie cutter to draw different shapes on foil and proceed*

¼ lb. white confection coating
Red food color
2 (8 or 9″) cake layers

2 cups white frosting
Silver dragées

Make 3 large and 8 small bell patterns of aluminum foil.

Coarsely grate white confection coating; melt over just simmering water until softened. Add just enough food color to make delicate pink. Using small spatula, spread coating on bell shapes; chill in freezer until set.

Put cake layers together with white frosting; frost sides and top of cake.

Carefully peel foil from bells. Place large bells in pattern on top of cake. Place small bells around sides of cake.

## THANKSGIVING CAKE

*If you wish, place the cornucopia on a layer cake. It will make a beautiful centerpiece for your Thanksgiving dinner table*

| | |
|---|---|
| 1 (13×9×2") cake | 1 sugar-type ice cream cone |
| 2 c. white frosting | (not waffle type) |
| 1 square unsweetened chocolate, | Marzipan fruits |
| melted | |

Frost sides and top of cake, reserving about ½ c. frosting for decoration.

Blend enough melted chocolate into the reserved frosting to make a good brown color. Frost ice cream cone; place on cake at attractive angle.

Using plain decorating tip, pipe appropriate greeting on top of cake. Place marzipan fruits on cake to pour out of cornucopia.

## PATRIOTIC CAKE

*What could be more perfect for a Fourth of July picnic or reunion*

| | |
|---|---|
| 2 c. white frosting | Red jelly |
| 2 (8 or 9") cake layers | Blue food color |

Set aside ½ c. frosting. With remaining frosting, put cake layers together and frost sides and top of cake. Using plain decorating tip, pipe around edge of cake and make squares on top of cake. Fill alternate squares with red jelly.

Color reserved frosting with blue food coloring. Using plain decorating tip, pipe stars in remaining squares with the frosting.

## GLAZED APRICOT CAKE

*Keep this beautiful golden cake refrigerated until serving time*

2 (8 or 9") white or sponge
round cake layers
1 (12 oz.) jar apricot preserves
(1 c.)

1½ c. orange-tinted or white
frosting
2 (1 lb.) cans apricot halves,
well-drained

Put cake layers together with ½ c. apricot preserves. Frost sides of cake with orange frosting. Using rosette decorating tip, place rosettes around edge of top of cake. Place apricot halves, rounded side up on top of cake.

Heat remaining apricot preserves just until melted; force through sieve to remove pulp. Spoon glaze over apricots.

## MOTHER'S DAY CAKE

*Delight mother on her special day with this attractive dessert*

2 c. fluffy white frosting
Red food color
2 (8 or 9") round cake layers
7 large red gumdrops

1 large purple gumdrop
3 large green gumdrops
1 large yellow gumdrop
Green decorating sugar

Tint frosting a delicate pink. Spread some of the frosting over one cake layer; top with remaining layer. Frost sides, then top of cake.

On well-sugared board, slightly roll red gumdrop to make a 2" circle. Snip in 4 places and shape into petals. Repeat with five red gumdrops and the purple gumdrop. Cut small pieces of yellow gumdrops to make centers. Cut 1 red gumdrop in half and roll each half to make flower buds. Roll out green gumdrops in long strips and cut into leaf shapes. Arrange 1 purple and 2 red flowers along with the 2 red buds and leaves in a decorative spray on top of cake. Place remaining 4 red flowers and leaves around bottom edge of cake. Sprinkle lightly with green decorating sugar as desired.

## SPRINGTIME CAKE

*You don't have to be an expert with a decorating tube to make this attractive cake which looks like a flower garden in spring*

1 (9") square cake
2 c. white frosting
1 (4¼ oz.) tube green
   decorating icing

Small pastel candy mints

Frost sides and top of cake with white frosting. Mark top of cake with 5 diagonal lines using a piece of string. Using a plain tip on decorating tube, pipe wavy lines over marked lines. Make small leaves at various intervals by drawing plain tip up quickly. Place pastel mints as desired.

## BIRTHDAY CAKE

*In no time, you'll be able to make a cake with a homemade touch*

2 (8 or 9") round cake layers
2 c. white frosting
Red licorice strings

4 jellied lemon slices
3 jellied orange slices
Assorted small gumdrops

Spread some of the frosting over one cake layer; top with remaining layer. Frost sides, then top of cake.

Shape licorice strings into loops around sides of cake. Work quickly while frosting is still soft.

Place a jellied lemon slice in center of cake. Shape a 4" strip of licorice to make a basket handle. Snip gumdrops into small pieces and arrange in basket like fruit. Cut remaining jellied slices into 6 wedges each and alternate yellow and orange wedges around edge of top.

## BUTTERFLY CAKE

*Welcome in spring with this lovely cake decorated with butterflies*

Green food color
1 tsp. water
1 (7 oz.) can flaked coconut
2 c. fluffy white frosting
Yellow food color

2 (8 or 9") round cake layers
Assorted large gumdrops
8 jellied slices of various colors
Black licorice strings

In a large jar dilute a few drops of green food color with water. Add coconut; cover and shake until evenly coated.

Tint frosting a delicate yellow. Spread some of the frosting over one cake layer: top with remaining layer. Frost sides, then top of cake.

To make butterfly body, shape one large gumdrop into a 1¼″ cylinder. Then place a jellied slice on each side of the cylinder for the wings. Cut short strips of black licorice strings to make feelers. Repeat. Place four butterflies on sides of cake. Sprinkle tinted coconut between butterflies.

On well-sugared board, slightly roll two orange gumdrops to make 2″ circles. Snip in 4 places and shape into petals. Cut small pieces of yellow gumdrops to make centers. Roll out green gumdrops in long strips and cut into leaf shapes. Arrange flowers and leaves in a decorative spray in center of cake. Sprinkle with tinted coconut around edge of top.

## WHEEL CAKE

*Just add some candles and you have a last-minute birthday cake*

2 (8 or 9″) round cake layers
2 c. white frosting
1 (6 oz.) pkg. chocolate
   nonpareils

1 (1¹¹⁄₁₆ oz.) chocolate flavor
   glossy decorating gel

Put cake layers together with frosting; frost sides and top of cake. Place nonpareils around bottom and top edge of sides of cake. Place more around top of cake and in center of top.

Using decorating gel, make lines between candies on sides of cake, and from center candy on top to those around edge.

N O T E : If desired, reserve some of frosting and color with melted chocolate rather than using gel.

## POP ART CAKE

*Frost cake pieces ahead like petits fours; let guests decorate pieces*

1 (1 lb. 2½ oz.) pkg. yellow cake mix
Pop Art Icing (recipe follows)
Decorations (red food color, light corn syrup, red cinnamon candies, red licorice "whips," colored decorating sugar, colored coconut)

Prepare cake mix according to package directions. Bake in 13×9×2″ pan; cool completely. Cut into 15 squares; brush off crumbs.

Place cakelets, one at a time, on wire rack over a large bowl. Pour Pop Art Icing over tops and sides of cakelets. Remove to clean racks to dry. Decorate iced cakelets in pop art designs. Tint ¼ c. leftover Pop Art Icing with red food color. Snip off tiny corner of clean, heavy envelope. Fill with tinted icing and seal well. Use as decorator tube.

Dot tops of cakelets with light corn syrup to stick on the red cinnamon candies and red licorice "whips." Brush cakelets with light corn syrup; sprinkle colored sugar and coconut evenly over the tops. Makes 15 servings.

**Pop Art Icing:** In top of double boiler, combine 2 (1 lb.) pkgs. confectioners sugar, sifted, ½ c. light corn syrup, ½ c. water, ½ tsp. almond extract and ¼ tsp. lemon extract. Beat until smooth. Stir over hot, not boiling, water until icing will pour freely. Keep icing over hot water while you decorate cakelets; stir frequently. To reuse icing, heat and stir over hot water. If it thickens, add water by teaspoonfuls and stir to keep at pouring consistency.

## MUG CAKES

*Serve these at graduation parties—they'll make a hit with the gang*

2 (17 oz.) pkgs. pound cake mix
1 (13 oz.) pkg. chocolate creamy-type frosting mix
1 (5¼ to 6½ oz.) pkg. white fluffy-type frosting mix

Cake decorations (8 red licorice "twisters," white mint patties and peppermint sticks)

Line bottoms and sides of 4 empty 1-lb. cans with waxed paper, allowing paper to extend 1″ over tops. Prepare 1 package pound cake mix according to package directions. Pour about 1 c. batter into each can.

Bake in slow oven (325°) 55 minutes, or until lightly browned. Cool 15 minutes in can, pull out cakes, remove papers.

Repeat, using second package of pound cake mix.

Prepare frosting mixes according to package directions. Frost sides with chocolate frosting, then tops with fluffy white frosting.

Stick white mint patties on sides of mugs and insert peppermint sticks.

Make mug handles by forcing ends of red licorice twisters into side of each cake.

To serve, cut each cake into vertical quarters. Makes 32 small pieces.

## "DON'T EAT THE DAISIES" DESSERT

Line a clay flowerpot (8" in diameter, 4¼" deep) with aluminum foil, making a double thickness of foil in the bottom. Grease foil lightly. Line bottom and sides of pot with lady finger halves (about 12 whole lady fingers).

Soften 3 pints orange sherbet and 1 pint lemon sherbet (or any 2 flavors of ice cream or sherbet you prefer) in 2 separate bowls; stir until smooth.

Spoon half of orange sherbet into bottom of pot, make a layer of lemon sherbet and spread remaining orange sherbet over lemon. Insert about 6 large straws, cut into 4" lengths into sherbet and place flower pot in freezer overnight.

Remove straws; turn out and invert dessert on serving plate. Replace straws. Mix ¼ c. confectioners sugar and 2 tblsp. cocoa; add ½ c. heavy whipping cream, ¼ tsp. vanilla. Whip. Spread on top of dessert.

Sprinkle with grated or shaved semisweet chocolate. Place dessert in freezer to firm. When ready to place on table, insert fresh flowers in straws. Let stand 15 minutes at room temperature for easier cutting. Makes 8 servings.

## HEREFORD CAKE

*Children of all ages will be enchanted with this whimsical cake made by transforming a lamb (mold) into a calf!*

| | |
|---|---|
| ½ c. butter or regular margarine | ½ tsp. vanilla |
| | ¼ tsp. lemon extract |
| 1½ c. sugar | 4 egg whites |
| 2½ c. sifted cake flour | Chocolate Frosting (recipe |
| 2 tsp. baking powder | follows) |
| ¼ tsp. salt | White Frosting (recipe follows) |
| 1 c. milk | |

Cream butter; add sugar gradually, beating until light and fluffy. Sift together dry ingredients; add to creamed mixture alternately with milk, beating to blend well. Beat in flavorings.

Beat egg whites until stiff but not dry; fold lightly into batter.

Grease both sides of cake mold (see note) very well; dust lightly with flour. Pour batter into the half of lamb cake mold containing face. (Use extra batter for about a dozen cupcakes.) Insert toothpick down in batter in nose area for reinforcement. Place other half of mold on top, making sure it "locks." Place mold on baking sheet; bake in moderate oven (350°) about 1 hour (about 25 minutes for cupcakes). Remove top of mold; let cool a few minutes then gently remove cake from mold. Stand up cake, propped from behind, until thoroughly cooled. Wrap and freeze, or cover and let stand overnight before frosting.

**Chocolate Frosting:** Blend together 3 c. sifted confectioners sugar and ⅓ c. soft butter or regular margarine; stir in 3 squares unsweetened chocolate, melted, 1½ tsp. vanilla and 3 to 4 tblsp. light cream or milk, just enough to make a good spreading consistency. Add 1 c. shredded coconut; blend.

**White Frosting:** Follow directions above, except omit chocolate. later for nose).

Set aside about 2 tblsp. frosting before adding coconut (to use

*To Decorate:* Partially thaw cake. Use small spatula to spread white frosting on face—build up hump on top of head or poll and make nose a rounded square with a little extra frosting. Frost neck, front of ears, front feet, tail switch and an area from top of head down back of neck to shoulders. Apply Chocolate Frosting to remainder of body. Make ears a little bigger and rounder and body a little fatter with extra frosting.

Add touch of red and touch of yellow food color with toothpick to the 2 tblsp. White Frosting to tint pink; apply in casual square for nose. Use raisins for eyes.

**Quick Variation:** Use 1 (1 lb. 1 oz.) pkg. pound cake mix. Make as directed on package and bake in mold. Use frosting mixes; add coconut to decorate.

NOTE: You can buy lamb cake molds in stores and they're listed in several mail order catalogs—under $2 for lightweight aluminum or $4 for cast aluminum. We made our recipe in a Maid of Scandinavia Co. mold (Minneapolis) ($2.25 for lightweight; $4 for cast aluminum).

## A WEDDING CAKE GOOD TO EAT

A gorgeous, tall wedding cake . . . a table aglow with silver . . . a room full of friends extending warm wishes . . . the reception is off to a good start. The cake is the important food for this festive occasion. And no other cake in the bride's life will ever mean so much to her. She wants it lovely to look at and delicious to taste. Too many wedding cakes, even though beautiful, are dry and tasteless.

To develop a recipe for a wedding cake that is handsome and delicious was the ambition of the home economists in our Test Kitchens. They wanted to perfect a recipe that is easy to follow and does not require the purchase of special pans for baking. Our Flower Wedding Cake is the result.

Along with the cake recipe, you will find two fillings (take your choice), and Fluffy White Frosting to cover the filled cake. Included are directions for assembling the cake in three tiers and for coating artificial flowers, the kind you buy at dime stores, by dipping them in a special frosting. The flowers provide the final touch of glory, the decoration.

You need no good luck charm to bake and decorate the cake successfully. Just follow the recipes and directions carefully and you'll find your production will rival the creations of the best and most expensive caterers. Here are suggestions on how to organize the work.

Dip the flowers in the sugar glaze (Dipping Frosting) a week before you bake the cake. Spread them in a box lined with waxed paper and store in a dry place.

Bake the cake and cool. Wrap at once in waxed paper to prevent drying.

Build the cake with your choice of fillings and spread with Sealing Frosting to keep down the crumbs. You can do this the day before the wedding. Or you can freeze the filled and sealed cake a week before frosting it.

Decide on the placement of the flowers. Then add the Fluffy White Frosting and the flowers on the wedding day.

This wedding cake is easy to cut, but here's a gracious way to do it. Lift off the top tier and save it for the bride and bridegroom. Cut the middle tier into 14 pieces; then cut the bottom tier into 36 rectangular pieces. Add them together and you'll have 50 servings.

Here are the recipes.

## FLOWER WEDDING CAKE

*You'll need to make two recipes of this cake to make the 3-tier beauty. Cake serves 50*

| | |
|---|---|
| 3⅓ c. sifted cake flour | ½ c. shortening |
| 4 tsp. baking powder | 1¾ c. sugar |
| 1½ tsp. salt | 1 egg yolk |
| 7 egg whites | 2 tsp. vanilla |
| ½ c. sugar | 1 tsp. almond extract |
| ½ c. butter | 1⅓ c. milk |

Pans are important. This cake *must* bake in shallow layers. Do not try to bake deeper cakes. Line 15½×10½×1″ jelly roll pan and 8″ square baking pan with plain brown paper. (*Do not* grease and flour pans, since this makes a crust that's too heavy.)

Sift cake flour, baking powder and salt together 3 times.

Beat egg whites until foamy. Add ½ c. sugar gradually; continue beating only until meringue will hold *soft* peaks. Set aside.

Cream butter and shortening together until well blended and smooth. Gradually add 1¾ c. sugar; beat until light and fluffy. Add the egg yolk and beat until well blended.

Add extracts to milk. Add milk alternately with dry ingredients to the creamed mixture, a small amount at a time; beat after each addition until smooth.

Add meringue and beat thoroughly into batter.

Spread batter in the two pans, about ½″ deep in each pan. Spread batter out to corners, leaving a slight depression in center. Tap pans sharply on counter top several times to remove large air bubbles.

Bake in moderate oven (350°) 25 to 30 minutes.

Cool on racks 10 minutes. Remove from pans and finish cooling on racks. To keep from drying, wrap as soon as cool.

## ALMOND CREAM FILLING AND SEALING FROSTING

*Take your pick of this or Orange/Raisin Filling—both luscious*

4 egg yolks, slightly beaten
1⅓ c. evaporated milk
1⅓ c. sugar
½ c. butter or regular
  margarine

2 tsp. vanilla
2 c. finely chopped toasted
  almonds

Blend yolks and milk in saucepan; stir in sugar and butter. Cook over medium heat, stirring constantly, until thick and bubbling. Add vanilla.

Remove 1½ c. of above cooked mixture and add to it 2 c. of finely chopped, toasted almonds. Cool; stir occasionally until of spreading consistency.

**Sealing Frosting:** Cool remainder of filling. Add 1½ to 2 c. sifted confectioners sugar and beat until of thin spreading consistency.


## ORANGE/RAISIN FILLING AND SEALING FROSTING

*Golden raisins and orange candy teamed with almonds*

½ c. sugar
2 tblsp. flour
2 c. golden raisins, ground
1 c. water

1 c. finely cut orange gumdrops
1 c. finely chopped toasted
  almonds

Combine sugar and flour. Add to raisins in saucepan. Add water and stir to dissolve. Cook, stirring constantly, until thick.

Add gumdrops and cook 3 minutes.

Add almonds and cool thoroughly before using.

**Sealing Frosting:** Blend 2 slightly beaten egg yolks with ⅔ c. evaporated milk in saucepan. Stir in ⅔ c. sugar and ¼ c. butter or regular margarine. Cook over medium heat, stirring constantly, until thick and bubbling.

Remove from heat; add 1 tsp. vanilla and cool.

Stir in 1½ to 2 c. sifted confectioners sugar and beat to thin spreading consistency.

*Bottom Tier:* Trim crusts from the two 15½×10½×1″ cakes to make smooth straight sides.

Cut 9½″ square and 4″ square from each cake. Reserve the 4″ squares for top tier. (You'll have some scraps.)

Cut 9½″ square of cardboard and cover with foil. Place 9½″ square of cake on cardboard. Spread desired filling evenly over cake top. Place other 9½″ cake square on filling and press firmly.

Spread thin layer of Sealing Frosting over sides and top of this tier. Pull spatula over surface to make smooth straight sides.

*Middle Tier:* Trim crusts from the two 8×8×2″ cakes to make 6½″ squares.

Cut 6½″ square of cardboard and cover with foil. Place 6½″ square of cake on cardboard. Spread with desired filling. Top with other 6½″ square of cake. Center 6½″ tier on bottom tier. Cover top and sides with Sealing Frosting.

*Top Tier:* Repeat procedure (using cardboard and foil) for two 4″ squares. Center this tier on middle tier. Seal top and sides with frosting.

## FLUFFY WHITE FROSTING

*Looks like a white satin cloud*

| | |
|---|---|
| 2 egg whites | ¼ tsp. cream of tartar |
| 1½ c. sugar | 1 tsp. vanilla |
| ⅓ c. water | |

Combine all ingredients, except vanilla, in top of double boiler. Beat 1 minute on high speed with electric mixer.

Place over boiling water. Cook 7 minutes, beating all the time on high speed with electric mixer.

Remove from hot water. Turn frosting into bowl. Add vanilla; beat until of spreading consistency.

**To Decorate Cake:** Let Sealing Frosting set before you apply Fluffy White Frosting.

Decide on placement of flowers before you apply final frosting.

Apply Fluffy White Frosting, starting with sides of bottom tier. Hold spatula perpendicular to tray and pull along carefully to make smooth sides and square corners. Apply to ledge of tier, building a ridge along outer edge. Repeat for each tier.

When frosting just begins to set, arrange flower design.

**To Make Decorations:** Select plastic flowers in pastel colors such as yellow or pink. For an orderly and attractive design, use no more than three varieties of flowers. Flowers that have definite form and petals that outline sharply show off best when dipped.

Wash plastic flowers in warm suds and rinse in clear water; dry. Cut individual flowers from stalk with a wire cutter, leaving a stem to hold when you dip it.

Dip plastic flowers in Dipping Frosting (recipe follows). Twirl in hand to distribute frosting evenly. Hold in hand a few minutes until frosting begins to set. Place on rack to dry. For thicker coating, you will probably want to dip again after first coating dries. When final coating is dry, snip off remaining stems.

Work out your desired arrangement for flowers before applying Fluffy White Frosting. Then when this final frosting is applied and just beginning to set, place flowers in desired spots.

## DIPPING FROSTING

| | |
|---|---|
| 2 c. sugar | 1 to 1½ c. sifted confectioners |
| 1 c. water | sugar |
| ⅛ tsp. cream of tartar | |

Combine 2 c. sugar, water and cream of tartar in saucepan. Cook to a thin syrup (226°). Remove from heat and cool to luke-warm (112°).

Add confectioners sugar gradually, stirring until smooth. Mixture should be of pouring consistency.

Place over warm water to keep frosting at right consistency for dipping. If too hot, plastic flowers will soften.

A little experimenting will determine the best consistency for coating. If you don't like appearance of flowers on first dipping, wash off frosting, pat dry with dish towel and redip.

## INFORMAL WEDDING CAKE

*You needn't be a caterer to bake this gorgeous cake—it's mix-made*

2 (18½ oz.) pkgs. white cake mix

2 recipes Fluffy White Frosting (recipe follows)

Marshmallow Flowers (recipe follows)

Miniature marshmallows (about 150)

Prepare 3-tier cake pan set (9", 7¼" and 5" by 1½" deep) by lining bottoms with plain paper.

Prepare one package of cake mix as directed on package. Pour ½ c. batter into small pan, 1 c. batter into next size pan and remaining batter into large pan. Spread evenly in pans. Tap pans sharply on table top to remove air pockets.

Bake small and medium layers in moderate oven (350°) about 20 minutes, the larger layer, 30 minutes. Cool on racks 5 minutes, then remove from pans. Brush crumbs from sides of cake while still warm. Complete cooling on racks.

Prepare batter from second package of cake mix in the same manner.

Make one recipe of Fluffy White Frosting. When cakes are cool, put layers of same size together with frosting, and coat sides and tops with a thin layer of frosting to seal the crumbs. Stack layers on each other; hold in place with thin skewers. Let stand until set. Meanwhile, make Marshmallow Flowers.

Prepare another recipe of Fluffy White Frosting. Remove skewers from cake; frost entire cake, starting at bottom tier and working up. Apply thickly around bottom tier. Draw small spatula over frosting to smooth it. Then make rides by pulling spatula in upward strokes all around. (If frosting seems to be crusting over quickly, do a small section at a time.) Pile frosting on bottom ledge and swirl around cake. Continue working up on the cake as directed for bottom tier. Pile and swirl frosting on top of cake.

Place miniature marshmallows in ridges in frosting, pressing firmly into frosting. Arrange Marshmallow Flowers on top of cake and around edge of plate for decoration. Makes 40 servings.

**Fluffy White Frosting:** Place 2 egg whites, 1½ c. sugar, ⅓ c. water, 2 tsp. light corn syrup and dash of salt in top of double boiler. Beat 1 minute with electric mixer or rotary beater. Cook over boiling water, beating constantly, until mixture stands in stiff peaks, about 7 minutes. Remove from heat. Transfer to mixing bowl; add 1 tsp. vanilla and beat until frosting is of good spreading consistency. Use at once. (You will need to make this frosting twice, once for filling and undercoat, again for final decoration.)

**Marshmallow Flowers:** Cut large marshmallows horizontally into 5 pieces, using kitchen scissors dipped in water. Attach these pieces as petals to a miniature marshmallow, used as a center. Dust fingers with confectioners sugar if pieces stick to fingers. Dip finished flower in colored sugar crystals.

# CHAPTER 9

# Frosty Ice Cream / Sherbet Coolers

When friends drop by unexpectedly or the children invite a parade of chums home for an after-school snack, bring out a tray filled with cool, nutritious ice cream drinks and a plate of homemade cake squares.

This chapter contains a colorful rainbow of drinks suitable for just about any occasion. There are long cool sippers with refreshing fruit bases, creamy floats, sparkling punches and bubbling ice cream sodas—depending on the ingredients you happen to have.

These recipes will give you a point of departure for many a way to serve new and different refreshments. For instance, why not have a Float-and-Soda Bar . . . let everyone "scoop and pour" his own creation? This would be a novel way to entertain at a children's birthday party, but teens and adults like the challenge, too. Cover a long table with a paper tablecloth. Line up your ingredients: chilled bottles of assorted flavored sodas, such as ginger ale, orange soda, strawberry and root beer; an assortment of ice cream and sherbet flavors; ice cream scoops, long plastic or metal spoons, colorful straws and tall glasses. Be sure to include a tray of glamorous garnishes such as fresh berries, pineapple chunks, lemon and lime slices, clusters of grapes, cinnamon and peppermint sticks and maraschino cherries. Then let the guests create their own drinks and help themselves to a piece of feathery light homemade cake.

## SPARKLING RED PUNCH

2 pkgs. *unsweetened* strawberry flavor instant soft drink mix

2 c. ice water

1 (16 oz.) can pineapple juice, chilled

1 (16 oz.) can frozen orange juice concentrate, thawed

1 (16 oz.) can frozen lemon juice concentrate, thawed

1 qt. lemon sherbet

1 (12 oz.) bottle strawberry soda, chilled

1 qt. carbonated water, chilled

Combine first 6 ingredients in a punch bowl; mix well. Just before serving, add strawberry soda and carbonated water. Makes about 16 to 20 servings.

## SUNNY ORANGE PUNCH

3 c. water
6 tea bags
4 tblsp. snipped mint leaves
½ c. light corn syrup
3 (6 oz.) cans frozen orange juice concentrate, thawed
⅓ c. lemon juice
1 pt. orange sherbet, softened
1 qt. ice cubes
2 qts. carbonated water
3 oranges, sliced
12 strawberries, sliced

Bring water to a full boil in saucepan. Remove from heat. Immediately add tea and mint. Brew, uncovered, for 4 minutes. Stir well. Strain into a large container. Cool.

Stir in corn syrup, orange juice concentrate, lemon juice and orange sherbet. Pour into punch bowl over ice cubes. Add carbonated water. Garnish with orange and strawberry slices. Makes about 4 quarts.

## CHRISTMAS CAROL PUNCH

2 qts. chilled Hawaiian Punch
2 qts. chilled cranberry juice
2 qts. black cherry soda, chilled
1 pt. cherry ice

Combine Hawaiian Punch and cranberry juice in a punch bowl. Add black cherry soda. Add scoops of cherry ice. Serve immediately. Makes about 6 quarts.

## COFFEE BANANA WHIP

2 bananas, cut in chunks
2 c. cold coffee
⅓ c. sugar
1 pt. coffee ice cream
2 tsp. vanilla

Combine all ingredients in blender container. Blend at high speed until thick and fluffy. Makes 6 servings.

## CREAMY BANANA NOG

3 eggs
3 bananas, cut in chunks
½ pt. vanilla ice cream
1 c. milk
2½ c. milk

Put eggs, bananas, ice cream and 1 c. milk in blender. Blend at high speed until smooth and creamy. Pour into pitcher or bowl and stir in 2½ c. milk. Pour into glasses. Serve with straws. Makes 6 servings.

## BANANA VELVET

2 c. milk
2 medium bananas, cut in
chunks

1 pt. banana ice cream, softened
Nutmeg

Put all ingredients in blender container. Cover and blend at high speed until smooth and creamy. Pour into chilled glasses. Sprinkle each serving with nutmeg. Serve with straws. Makes 6 servings.

## FRESH ORANGE/GINGER FLOAT

1½ c. fresh orange juice, chilled
2 (12 oz.) cans ginger ale

1 pt. chocolate ice cream
4 tsp. grated orange peel

Mix orange juice and ginger ale; pour into tall glasses. Scoop ice cream into glasses and sprinkle orange peel on top. Serve with straws and soda spoons. Makes 6 servings.

## HONEY ORANGE FLIP

2 c. orange juice, chilled
2 c. milk
3 eggs
⅓ c. honey

1 medium banana, cut in
pieces
1 pt. vanilla ice cream
Maraschino cherries with stems

Put first five ingredients in blender container. Cover and blend at high speed until smooth. Pour into tall glasses over cracked ice. Top each serving with a small scoop of vanilla ice cream. Garnish with a maraschino cherry. Makes 6 servings.

## ORANGE BREEZE

3 c. orange juice
2 tblsp. lemon juice
1 pt. vanilla ice cream, softened

1 pt. orange sherbet, softened
Orange slices
Fresh mint

Pour orange and lemon juice in blender container. Spoon in ice cream and sherbet. Cover and blend on low speed until smooth. Pour into tall glasses over cracked ice. Garnish with an orange slice and sprig of mint. Makes 6 servings.

## CREAMY COFFEE FROSTED

4 qts. cold coffee
1 qt. milk
1 tblsp. vanilla

1 c. sugar
2 qts. vanilla ice cream, softened

Combine cold coffee, milk and vanilla. Add sugar and stir to dissolve. Chill thoroughly. Pour over ice cream in punch bowl. Makes 30 punch-cup servings.

## COFFEE FLOAT

1 (3½ oz.) pkg. instant vanilla
   pudding
¼ c. instant coffee powder or
   granules

5 c. milk
1 pt. coffee walnut ice cream
Cinnamon

Combine pudding mix and instant coffee in a large bowl. Add ½ c. of the milk. Blend thoroughly. Slowly add remaining milk, blending well. Beat with a rotary beater for 1 minute. Chill. Stir just before serving. Pour into chilled coffee mugs. Top each serving with a scoop of coffee walnut ice cream and sprinkle lightly with cinnamon. Makes 6 servings.

## COFFEE BUTTERSCOTCH

¾ c. prepared butterscotch
   topping
½ c. light cream

4 c. cold coffee
1 pt. coffee ice cream

Combine ingredients in a large bowl of electric mixer. Beat until frothy. Pour into tall glasses. Serve at once. Makes 6 servings.

## PEACH FROSTED

1 c. chilled sliced peaches, fresh
   or canned
1 c. milk

¼ tsp. almond extract
1 pt. peach ice cream
2 c. milk

Combine peaches, 1 c. milk, almond extract and peach ice cream in blender container. Cover. Blend at high speed until smooth and creamy. Pour into bowl or pitcher. Stir in 2 c. milk. Pour into chilled glasses. Makes 6 servings.

## RASPBERRY FLING

| | |
|---|---|
| 3 (3 oz.) pkgs. raspberry flavor gelatin | 2¼ c. orange juice |
| 4 c. boiling water | 1¼ c. lemon juice |
| 1½ c. sugar | 1 qt. ginger ale |
| 4 c. cold water | 2 (10 oz.) pkgs. frozen raspberries |
| ½ c. lime juice | 1 qt. raspberry sherbet |

Dissolve gelatin in boiling water; add sugar, cold water and juices; cool, but do not chill or gelatin will congeal. (If you let it congeal, heat just enough to bring back to liquid state.)

When time to serve, pour punch into punch bowl. Add ginger ale and frozen raspberries. Stir until raspberries break apart and are partially thawed. Top with scoops of raspberry sherbet. Makes about 4 quarts.

## GOLDEN COOLER

| | |
|---|---|
| 1 (6 oz.) can frozen orange juice concentrate | 1 c. pineapple juice |
| 1 c. grapefruit juice | 1 pt. pineapple sherbet |

Reconstitute orange juice concentrate according to directions on can. Combine with grapefruit and pineapple juice in a large bowl Pour over cracked ice in tall glasses. Top each serving with a small scoop of pineapple sherbet. Makes 6 servings.

## GRAPE FRAPPE

| | |
|---|---|
| 1½ c. grape juice | 2 c. evaporated milk |
| 2 tsp. lemon juice | 2 c. water |
| ⅓ c. sugar | 1 pt. grape ice cream |

Combine grape juice, lemon juice and sugar in a large bowl; mix well. Gradually beat in milk that has been combined with the water. Beat in ice cream. Pour into tall glasses over cracked ice. Makes 6 servings.

## CRANBERRY QUENCHER

2 qts. cranberry juice
2 c. light corn syrup
1 qt. ice cubes

1 qt. lemon-lime soda
1 qt. creamy lime sherbet

Combine cranberry juice and corn syrup in a punch bowl. Chill. Just before serving, add ice cubes and lemon-lime soda. Top with scoops of lime sherbet. Makes about 25 servings.

## TRIPLE FRUITED COOLER

1 (6 oz.) can frozen orange juice concentrate, thawed
1 qt. apple juice, chilled
1 pt. strawberry sherbet

Combine thawed concentrate and apple juice in a large bowl. Beat until well blended. Pour into tall glasses over cracked ice. Top each serving with a small scoop of strawberry sherbet. Makes 6 to 8 servings.

## LEMONY GRAPE COOLER

2 c. grape juice
Juice of 2 lemons
Juice of 2 oranges

1 (12 oz.) can ginger ale
1 pt. lemonade ice cream

Combine fruit juices. Just before serving, add ginger ale. Pour over ice cubes in glasses. Top with small scoops of ice cream. Makes 6 servings.

## NECTAR BREEZE

3 (12 oz.) cans apricot nectar, chilled
2 bananas, thinly sliced
1½ c. strawberry sherbet

Pour nectar into tall glasses. Add banana and top each glass with spoonfuls of sherbet. Makes 6 servings.

## CHOCOLATE SODA

1 (1 lb.) can chocolate flavored
    syrup
½ c. light cream

2 pts. chocolate mint ice cream
2 qts. carbonated water

Into 6 (12 oz.) glasses, pour 3 tblsp. chocolate syrup. Stir in 1 tblsp. light cream. Add 2 small scoops chocolate mint ice cream. Add carbonated water to fill each glass; stir lightly. Serve immediately. Makes 6 servings.

## STRAWBERRY/PINEAPPLE SODA

2 (10 oz.) pkgs. frozen
    strawberries, thawed
2 (13½ oz.) cans pineapple
    chunks, drained

2 pts. strawberry ice cream
1 pt. vanilla ice cream
1 qt. carbonated water

Drain strawberries and reserve juice. Combine strawberries and pineapple. Into 6 (12 oz.) glasses, pour ⅓ c. combined fruit mixture. Add 2 tblsp. strawberry juice. Add 1 small scoop strawberry ice cream.

Add ⅓ c. combined fruit mixture and add 1 tblsp. strawberry juice. Top with a small scoop each of vanilla ice cream and strawberry ice cream.

Add carbonated water to fill each glass; stir lightly. Serve immediately. Makes 6 servings.

## ORANGE SODA

4 (6 oz.) cans frozen orange
    juice concentrate, thawed
½ c. light cream

1 qt. ginger ale
1 pt. vanilla ice cream
1 pt. orange sherbet

Into 6 (12 oz.) glasses, pour ½ c. orange juice concentrate. Add 1 tblsp. light cream; mix well.

Stir in ¼ c. ginger ale. Add 1 small scoop each of vanilla ice cream and orange sherbet.

Add ginger ale to fill each glass; stir lightly. Serve immediately. Makes 6 servings.

## FROSTED MOCHA

2 c. cold coffee
1 c. cocoa, chilled
1 pt. coffee ice cream, softened

Combine cold coffee, cocoa and ice cream. Beat thoroughly with blender or beater until smooth and foamy. Pour into tall glasses. Makes 4 to 5 servings.

## MILK SHRUB

1 qt. milk
3 pts. orange sherbet
1 qt. grapefruit soda, chilled

Combine milk and 2 pts. sherbet. Beat until smooth; add soda; stir gently, just until blended.

Pour into chilled glasses or punch bowl; spoon remaining sherbet on top. Makes 14 tall glasses or 28 half-cup servings.

N O T E : You may substitute lime or raspberry sherbet for orange. Or use lemon-lime soda instead of grapefruit.

# INDEX